Golf Playoffs

Golf Playoffs

A Sourcebook of Major Championship Men's and Women's Amateur and Professional Playoffs, 1876–1990

by
DAVID G. MARRANDETTE

McFarland & Company, Inc., Publishers
Jefferson, North Carolina, and London

REF
870 89174

British Library Cataloguing-in-Publication data are available

Library of Congress Cataloguing-in-Publication Data

Marrandette, David G., 1947–
    Golf playoffs : a sourcebook of major championship men's and
women's amateur and professional playoffs, 1876–1990 / by David G.
Marrandette.
        p.   cm.
    Includes bibliographical references and index.
    ISBN 0-89950-552-X (lib. bdg. : 55# alk. paper) ∞
    1. Golf—Tournaments—History.   I. Title.
GV970.M36   1991
796.352′6—dc20
                                                                90-53506
                                                                CIP

Manufactured in the United States of America

McFarland & Company, Inc., Publishers
    Box 611, Jefferson, North Carolina 28640

Acknowledgments

I would like to acknowledge my fellow golfer and golfwriter Nevin Gibson from the Archives of Golf for his immense contribution. Nevin provided all of the pictures found in this book. Without his assistance this volume would be mere words.

I would also like to thank the many people who freely gave a few minutes of their time to allow an interview. Of great assistance was Betty Dodd, former LPGA Tour player and now an official with the Texas State Golf Association. She provided valuable information on the early days of the LPGA Tour.

Contents

Part I. MEN

1
Introduction

Golf, like no other sport, epitomizes the dramatic in the manner it employs to resolve ties for its championships, especially the major championships. The competition is made unique by the fact that during the regulation play of the tournament the player competes against the entire field. But when a tie occurs after four rounds of against-the-entire-field competition, a head-to-head confrontation is established to determine the winner.

While parallels can be drawn between bowling and golf, much of the tournament proper in bowling consists of head-to-head competition, even down to the title match of a tournament. Only in golf, when a playoff ensues, does the format change and the outcome ultimately hinges on a head-to-head duel.

In all of sport no such drama is reproduced. Even the tie-breaker system used in tennis is not an equitable comparison. The tête-à-tête of the golf playoff remains the only major sports competition in which one player's physical action does not directly affect the response of the other. At no point in the head-to-head confrontation does one player have to specifically react to another's action. His options always remain the same, no matter what the outcome of another player's shot. No other major sport pits player against player, shot against shot to decide the victor.

The drama of the moment is heightened by the length of the playoff. There is an adverse effect. The shorter the playoff, the more immediate and intense the drama. And conversely, the longer the playoff, the more time the crescendo has to build.

The length of playoffs in the major championships of golf has deviated greatly through the years. Even now it remains diverse among the four major championships of professional golf. Currently, only the PGA and the Masters have the same playoff format, a hole-by-hole sudden-death. The U.S. Amateur and the British

Amateur are both currently conducted at match play and thus do not afford the opportunity for a playoff.

This constant fluctuation in the length of playoffs has been influenced by the state of the game at that particular moment in time and by the environment surrounding the tournament. As modern technology has increased, so has the demand for a same-day champion. The chief influence has, of course, been television. As of today, only the men's and women's U.S. Open Championships hold fast to an eighteen hole playoff on the following day.

When the first British Open playoff was required in 1883, it was held at thirty-six holes. Not coincidentally, this was also the length of the tournament itself at that time. By 1963 the playoff length had been reduced to eighteen holes. Finally, in 1984 the Royal and Ancient opted for a modified sudden-death format, a formula that went untested until 1989.

In 1895, when the U.S. Open was inaugurated at Newport, Rhode Island, an eighteen hole playoff scheduled for the following day was adopted to resolve ties for the championship. At one point in the late 1920s the USGA decided that a thirty-six hole playoff was the proper length for determining the champion. Eventually this led to a marathon seventy-two hole playoff in 1931. Not surprisingly, by 1939 the playoff length had reverted back to eighteen holes.

In 1935, the second year of the Masters and the first year of a playoff in that event, officials opted for a thirty-six hole confrontation. By 1942 the format had changed to an eighteen hole playoff and in 1979 officials elected to use the sudden-death blueprint beginning at the tenth hole.

The PGA Championship, when it converted to a stroke play tournament in 1958, initially utilized an eighteen hole playoff to settle all ties. It has only been in recent years that the sudden-death playoff has been adopted.

The U.S. Amateur, which was conducted as a stroke play championship from 1964 to 1972, also employed the eighteen hole playoff during its short duration as a medal play tournament.

Virtually all of the great players in the history of the game have been involved in playoffs for a major championship. The list of winners and losers reads like a who's who of major championship golf. From Willie Anderson to Tom Watson, from Bobby Jones to Jack Nicklaus, from Harry Vardon to Arnold Palmer—all have left a special mark on championship playoffs.

Almost without exception, major championships are fittingly, as might be expected, played over renowned and legendary courses. Of the four major championships for men only the Masters is played annually over the same course. To maintain the integrity and tradition of its championship, the Royal and Ancient uses a rotation of courses for the British Open. Although the USGA does not employ the rigid, tradition-bound rotation of the R and A, it still periodically returns its championship to the classically designed and traditional courses of the United States. And the PGA, while it has in the past occasionally chosen weak courses, schedules its competition to be conducted on courses that will provide a stern test for the professional golfer.

Each of the major championships offers a different venue for the aspiring champion. The British Open is routinely played over links courses that are natural in their setting and susceptible to the elements. The U.S. Open is known for its narrow fairways, thick rough, and lightning fast greens. The PGA generally emulates the USGA but usually with a lesser degree of severity; opting for better scores, but still punishing poor play or a lack of good judgment. And the Augusta National Golf Club, home of the Masters, is characterized by wide fairways and large, undulating greens that demand exact placement with the approach shot.

When evaluating the historical significance of a playoff in a major championship, several factors must be considered.

Timing. The outcome of the playoff in correlation with the calendar of world events and the present status of the game itself is paramount in the determination of historical significance. While each playoff has a certain importance, some are more noteworthy simply because of their timing.

Participants. Directly connected to the timing of a playoff are the participants. The players involved, taking into account their import and standing in the game both at the time of the playoff and many years henceforth, are key factors in ascertaining the mark a playoff leaves on the world of golf.

The distinction of the participants is of the utmost concern. A clash between two already established stars of the game may qualify as a "classic" confrontation. When a decided underdog is involved, there may be a "David and Goliath" effect. And, if the underdog wins, the immediate and long-term effects must be judged.

Human interest may also provide a valuable piece of the

puzzle, particularly if the victor of the playoff is a dark horse. The circumstances surrounding his victory must be examined in order to fully appreciate its meaning.

Since all the pieces of this puzzle may not fit until many years later, a playoff occurring in recent history may have to be periodically reevaluated as the years progress. For example, if a player loses a playoff for a major championship early in his career, does that loss affect his golf adversely or positively in later years?

Play. Some playoffs become noteworthy solely due to the quality of play. Usually this factor points to exceptionally remarkable play, but it can also be significant in the light of extremely poor quality. And very often the play of the final holes in regulation bears upon the final significance of the playoff. Just how the tie occurred can be just as notable as how the tie was resolved.

Other factors, although carrying secondary importance, should also be considered. The reputation or quality of the course involved can lend some historical or legendary interest to the playoff. Weather conditions that were endured throughout the tournament and the playoff could further affect the outcome of the event.

There can be no question that playoffs in major championships have left their mark on the game. A review and examination of each produces a microcosm of the game itself.

2
British Open

Since 1919 the Royal and Ancient Golf Club of St. Andrews, Scotland, has been responsible for the administration of the British Open. The Open, as it is commonly referred to outside the United States, is the oldest of the four major championships. The inaugural event was conducted in 1860 over the twelve holes of the links of Prestwick on the west coast of Scotland and was conducted solely for professional golfers, eight of whom participated. The prize for victory in the competition was "The Champion Belt," made of red Morocco leather and silver. The following year the tournament was opened to amateurs as well as professionals and became the first true open championship.

The first thirty-one championships were conducted at stroke play over thirty-six holes. The initial twelve were held at Prestwick, three times around the twelve hole layout of the historic links. There was no tournament in 1871, the year after Young Tom Morris had retired the championship belt with three consecutive victories (1868–70). When the championship resumed in 1872, this time in competition for The Cup, Young Tom won again for a fourth consecutive title, a feat that has never been duplicated. Eventually, in 1892, the British Open was changed to seventy-two holes of stroke play where it remains today.

Yet, despite its long history, only 13 of the 118 British Open championships through 1989 have resulted in a tie, thus requiring a playoff. The first occurred in 1876, the last in 1989, 14 years removed from the previous playoff in 1975.

Strangely, of the twenty-four British Open championships held at Prestwick, none required a playoff. St. Andrews, which has hosted the British Open twenty-three times, has been the site of the most playoffs in the Open—four.

The British Open has a varied history in the duration of its

The R and A golf clubhouse. The cornerstone was laid in 1852 and the spiritual home for all golfers was completed in 1854.

playoffs. Initially, when the length of the championship proper was thirty-six holes, all played in one day, a playoff of another thirty-six holes the following day was required to break the tie. This occurred twice. In 1892, when the British Open was expanded to seventy-two holes over two days, the playoff length remained at thirty-six holes.

From 1970 to 1984 playoff winners were determined by an eighteen hole playoff. This format witnessed only two playoffs, in 1970 and 1975.

Finally, in 1984 a system was devised and instituted to end the tournament on the final day of regulation play with the adoption of a unique tie-breaking method. The Royal and Ancient determined that, henceforth, playoffs would be conducted over a four or five hole stretch, the number and order being determined by the course layout. The player with the lowest aggregate score over the set number of holes would be declared the winner. If a deadlock still remained, the championship would then be settled in a hole-by-hole sudden-death. Royal and Ancient officials believe this format is the most expedient and equitable in that it favors neither the player who is sitting in the clubhouse nor the player just off the course, while at the same time deciding the outcome on the same day. The 1989 championship was the first time that this playoff blueprint was tested.

1876: St. Andrews, Scotland

This, the sixteenth British Open and the second Open held at St. Andrews, involved a most unusual controversy in determining the winner of the championship.

David Strath, a runner-up in both the 1870 and 1872 British Opens, and Robert Martin, one of the premier players of the day, tied at the end of regulation play with scores of 176. But, before a playoff could be arranged, a complaint was entered against Strath claiming that he had broken the rules by hitting his approach to the seventeenth green while the players ahead were still putting, allegedly striking one of them. (At that time, this action was against the rules.) And to further compound the matter, the players were not British Open participants.

In the formative days of the Open the organization was quite casual, even to the extent that the course itself was not set aside strictly for the play of the championship. Thus the competitors mingled in with the local folk out for a casual game of their own.

Strath, overtly the defensive type, became disgruntled with the complaint itself and the amount of time consumed by the tournament committee to decide the issue. He forthrightly refused a playoff and Martin was declared the winner by default—after he himself had walked the course to make the result official.

Strath was a bold and brash gentleman to say the least. In that same year, 1876, he sponsored himself to go around the links of St. Andrews under the moonlight in less than 100 strokes. In typical Strath-like fashion he finished in 95 without losing a ball.

1883: Musselburgh, Scotland

In the first actual occurrence of a playoff in British Open history, Willie Fernie of St. Andrews defeated Robert Ferguson of the host club by a single stroke in a second thirty-six holes, 158 to

159, after both had recorded scores of 159 for the thirty-six holes of the tournament proper.

Fernie's playoff victory was accomplished in sensational and dramatic style. Trailing Ferguson by a single shot coming to the final hole, Fernie drove the green on the short ninth and holed the putt for an eagle two against Ferguson's par four to win by one shot. Fernie's dramatics foiled Ferguson's bid to win the Open championship for the fourth consecutive year.

1889: Musselburgh, Scotland

Again the links of Musselburgh, one of the first homes for the Honourable Company of Edinburgh Golfers, were the scene for the second actual playoff in British Open history. This was the final Open championship to be played over the Musselburgh course.

Musselburgh has a distinguished history in the British Open by virtue of its early tradition. When the early organizers of the Open decided to move the tournament outside the sole realm of Prestwick after the 1872 championship, Musselburgh, along with Prestwick and St. Andrews, became one of the three venues for the championship. The course was host to six championships, 1874, 1877, 1880, 1883, 1886, and 1889. Today it no longer exists and is now home to a racetrack. Following this finale at Musselburgh, the Honourable Company moved and took with it the Open championship.

Originally the course had but seven holes, but in the mid–1880s two more were added, making the length 2,850 yards for the nine hole layout — still quite short for a championship layout, even in the days of the gutta-percha. Yet it was here that the six Opens at Musselburgh were played. The course was short yet tricky. The few hazards that were present were strategically placed, thus forcing a right way and a wrong way to play the hole.

In the tournament proper Willie Park, Junior, playing on his home course, thrilled the hometown fans when he came from two shots down with three to play to record a thirty-six hole total of 155 which tied Andrew Kirkaldy.

In the playoff, which took place three days later owing to an lack of urgency on the part of the organizing committee, Park took control early and led by three at the end of the first eighteen holes and stretched his margin of victory to five at the end, 158 to 163.

Park, Junior, came from the finest of golfing stock. His father, Willie Park, Senior, had won four British Open championships, including the inaugural event in 1860 and his uncle, Mungo, had won the title in 1874.

Willie Park, Junior, eventually became the first professional of his day to develop interests outside of playing and making equipment. He was the first professional to write about the game in *The Game of Golf,* and was also the first professional to try his hand at course design, Sunningdale in England being his most famous creation.

1896: Muirfield, Scotland

The playoff for the 1896 British Open title marks the first playoff confrontation between two legends of the game and the first and only playoff conducted at Muirfield.

Muirfield is the home of the Honourable Company of Edinburgh Golfers, the longest continuing club of golfers in the world. As a golf course, it is eminently fair. The fairways are well designed with ample bunkers to catch the errant shot. The greens are encased in bunkers that are all clearly visible to the player. While it is not a links course according to the strictest definition of the term, that is, it is not set hard against the sea, Muirfield still maintains many of the qualities of linksland golf.

In the seventy-two hole tournament of 1896, Harry Vardon, winner of a record six titles in the event, and John Henry Taylor, a five-time British Open champion, tied at 316.

The final hole of regulation provided insight into Vardon's style of play and his theories on golf course management. Needing a par four on Muirfield's difficult eighteenth to secure a victory, Vardon struck a solid drive, but was faced with a dilemma for his second. With a perfect second shot he could clear a dangerous greenside bunker and most assuredly make par. But with the slightest mishit, he could easily make six and lose the tournament altogether. Vardon elected to lay up short of the bunker and made five to tie Taylor.

The playoff, however, did not take place immediately on the next morning. Resulting from a quirk in scheduling, the playoff was postponed for one day to allow for participation in a professional tournament scheduled in North Berwick, just a few miles south. Vardon and Taylor competed at North Berwick and then returned to Muirfield the following day for the thirty-six hole playoff.

When the playoff finally did ensue, Vardon jumped to a quick five-shot lead after six holes. But Taylor came back with some sterling golf of his own and eventually nibbled the lead to one, finally settling for a two-stroke deficit at the end of the first eighteen. As the afternoon round began, Vardon lost his advantage immediately when he pulled his tee shot out of bounds on the par-three first. Nevertheless, he quickly recovered, gaining a stroke on each of the next three holes. That margin was all Vardon needed as he went on to win by four shots, 157 to 161.

Years later Vardon credited his putter as the key to his victory in the playoff. This "key to victory" was a new putter he had procured in North Berwick on that intervening day before the playoff. Vardon had visited the golf shop of club maker Ben Sayers. Coming upon an old cleek that looked perfect to the eye, he had a shorter shaft installed and declared the club a putter, the key that opened the door to the first of six British Open championships.

Vardon was, perhaps, the first great superstar of the game. His impact on the game at the turn of the century extended to both sides of the ocean. He learned the game caddying as a young boy and made his first appearance in the British Open in 1893, the same year as Taylor's inaugural British Open. From 1896 to 1922 he appeared in twenty-two consecutive championships, amassing eighteen top ten finishes. In 1914 he recorded his sixth victory in the event.

Vardon, however, is best remembered in the United States for two distinct reasons. First, he was the man who universalized the overlapping grip. Second, he was one of the two primary protagonists to Francis Ouimet's playoff victory in the 1913 U.S. Open.

J. H. Taylor, a member of golf's first "Great Triumvirate" along with Vardon and James Braid, turned to golf after all else failed. He was rejected for military service because of poor eyesight and later turned away from the police force because he was too short. He turned professinal at age nineteen.

He won the first of his five Open titles in 1894 at Sandwich, and the last at the age of forty-two in 1913 at Hoylake. He died at the age of ninety-two in February 1963, the last survivor of the Great Triumvirate.

1911: Royal St. George's, England

Harry Vardon defeated Arnaud Massy in a scheduled thirty-six hole playoff when Massy conceded after the thirty-fifth hole. The pair had tied after seventy-two holes with totals of 303. This was Vardon's fifth of six victories in the British Open.

Of the eleven British Open championships that have been played at Royal St. George's, only the 1911 event and the 1949 tournament required a playoff. The club was founded by Scotsman Laidlaw Purves and a few friends in 1887. The course is set amidst the dunes and tall grasses between the town of Sandwich and the sea on the Kent coast. The difficulty in the course is found in its uneven lies and the constant wind which makes each shot a unique challenge.

Royal St. George's is steeped in golf history. In 1904 the American Walter Travis became the first foreigner to win a British championship, the British Amateur. In 1922 Walter Hagen became the first U.S. born player to capture the British Open. And in 1930 Bobby Jones, in the year of his Grand Slam led a U.S. Walker Cup team to victory at Royal St. George's.

Arnaud Massy was the first great player from continental Europe. Four years earlier Massy had gained the distinction of becoming both the first foreign winner and the first continental winner of the Open, a feat not duplicated until 1979 when Seve Ballesteros won at Royal Lytham and St. Anne's.

Massy was a stockily built man who possessed a deft putting touch. While he never won another major championship, he amassed an astonishing number of victories in the open championships of several countries. He won the French Open in 1906 and 1907 and the Belgian Open in 1910. Massy's last important triumph came in the 1928 Spanish Open at the age of fifty-one.

1921: St. Andrews, Scotland

In 1921 the second of four playoffs at St. Andrews took place between Jock Hutchison, a native of St. Andrews playing out of the Glenview Club in Chicago, and Roger Wethered, the only amateur involved in a playoff for the Open title. Both recorded scores of 296 at the end of regulation play.

Hutchison had begun his homecoming early, arriving at St.

Andrews in the winter to begin his preparations. By the time the championship began, he was ready, if not, perhaps, overly ready.

In the tournament proper he remained in contention through fifty-four holes, despite a third round 79 that left him four strokes behind the leaders and one behind Wethered.

But in the final round Wethered shot 71, a score that demanded a three under par 70 from Hutchison in order to tie. After a 36 going out, Hutchison's task looked formidable, if not impossible. But Jock saved his best for last, scoring 34, while just missing a birdie on the last for an outright win.

In the thirty-six hole playoff Hutchison had little trouble with the amateur scoring 74–76—150 to win by nine shots. He was the first golfer to take the British Open cup to the United States.

During the tournament proper and much to the delight of his hometown fans, Hutchison established a British Open scoring record that still stands to this day, three strokes in two consecutive holes. In successive holes Hutchison scored a hole-in-one and a two, with the second being only inches away from a second consecutive ace.

1933: St. Andrews, Scotland

In the first all-American playoff for the British Open title, Denny Shute defeated Craig Wood after the two had deadlocked at 292 over seventy-two holes. During the tournament proper, Shute produced one of those odd moments in golf scoring 73 in all four rounds and making him the first and only Open champion with four identical rounds.

The thirty-six hole playoff had an ill-fated beginning for Wood. On the par-four first hole he hit his second into the Swilcan Burn that fronts the green. Electing to play the ball from the water, Wood removed his shoes and socks and proceeded to splash and slash his way to a double-bogie six, losing two shots to Shute. He then lost two more on the second. The remainder of the playoff was played almost dead even and Shute won by five, 149 to 154.

This was to be the first of three consecutive major championship playoffs in which Wood was a participant. He lost them all.

1949: Royal St. George's, England

The Open, like most other major sporting events, seems to draw some controversy from time to time, and those disputes are magnified by the significance of the event.

In 1949 after South African Bobby Locke and Harry Bradshaw had tied for the championship at 283, the scheduled playoff nearly did not come about. Locke refused to participate in the playoff until the flag positions were changed. At that time it was common practice to leave the holes in the same position for the entire week.

When the thirty-six hole playoff finally did ensue, Locke easily took the measure of Bradshaw, 135 to 147, the largest margin of victory ever in a British Open.

Acclaimed as one of the greatest putters of all times, Locke was the first world-class golfer to emerge from South Africa. However, Locke was not only committed to golf, but also to patriotism. During World War II he shunned golf for two and one-half years, serving as a bomber pilot in the South African Air Force. His 1949 playoff victory was the first of four Open titles for the likable South African.

1958: Royal Lytham and St. Anne's, England

In the first playoff at Royal Lytham and St. Anne's, Australian Peter Thomson defeated Welshman Dave Thomas over thirty-six holes, 139 (68, 71) to 143 (69, 74).

Founded in 1886, the course is quite unique as courses for the British Open are concerned. From its fairways, many of which are enclosed by houses, one is unable to view the sea. It is varied in its layout beginning with a par three, quite unusual for a championship course. But the real challenge of Royal Lytham is the inward nine with its constant changing of directions challenged by a prevailing westerly wind. On a course with driving accuracy at a premium, this demands all of a player's skill.

In 1958 the tournament proper ended in a mad scramble. Eric Brown needed only a par four in the final hole for a total of 277 that would have given him an outright victory by one shot. He took six and finished third. Thomson and Thomas, who were playing behind Brown, both made four on the final hole for totals of 278.

Even then, behind this pairing came the Irishman Christy O'Connor and the Argentinian Leopoldo Ruiz, both needing fours on the last to tie. O'Connor could do no better than five after bunkering his second and Ruiz made seven, failing on three attempts to remove his ball from a separate greenside bunker.

For Thomson the victory marked his fourth of five British Open championships. From 1954 to 1865 he accumulated an astonishing total of five British Open titles. Although four of his championship victories occurred at a period when the best competition from the United States elected to pass up the British Open, he nevertheless faced stiff competition from the likes of South African Bobby Locke, Britons Dai Rees and Eric Brown, and Belgian Flory van Donck. When he won his fifth title in 1965, the Americans had "rediscovered" the British Open and were prominent in the competition.

While it is arguable, considering the records and television-related popularity of David Graham and Greg Norman, Thomson could be considered the best player to have emerged from Australia. He won his first tournament as a professional, the 1950 New Zealand Open, a championship he won eight more times.

Thomson's strength was in his ability to manage his game and the golf course. His success in the Open was due to the fact that he never beat himself.

1963: Royal Lytham and St. Anne's, England

Bob Charles of New Zealand became the first and only left-hander to win a major championship when he easily defeated American Phil Rodgers in a thirty-six hole playoff, 140 to 148. In the playoff both of Charles's rounds were under par, a 69 and a 71. The pair had tied at the end of regulation with 277 totals, just one shot off the record established by Arnold Palmer one year earlier.

Charles, whose parents are also left-handed golfers, is the sole world-class player that New Zealand has produced and the only player from his country to win a major championship. In 1954 at the age of eighteen, while still an amateur, Charles won the New Zealand Open by one stroke over Bruce Crampton and two over Peter Thomson, the reigning British Open champion. Nevertheless, Charles did not turn professional for another six years.

Significantly, this was the last thirty-six hole playoff in major championship golf. By 1963 the Masters, U.S. Open, and the PGA had all reverted to eighteen hole playoffs to decide ties.

1970: St. Andrews, Scotland

Jack Nicklaus won an emotional playoff victory over Doug Sanders, the sympathetic choice of the fans. In what has become the most infamous putt in British Open history, Sanders missed from three feet on the seventy-second green with a stroke that tried to wish the ball in more than stroke it. That putt would have given him the outright championship in regulation play at 282.

In the playoff Sanders maintained his composure quite well, considering the events of the previous day. Yet Nicklaus stood on the eighteenth tee with a one-shot lead and a following wind. Not wanting to let the championship get away and playing slightly to the dramatic, Nicklaus removed his sweater and unleashed a blow that landed just short of the green, and bounced over into the rough behind.

Sanders, famous for his "phone booth" swing and colorful dress, pitched his second shot to four feet, forcing Nicklaus to execute a difficult chip to a sloping green. His chip came up eight feet short, but in typical Nicklaus fashion he sank the sharply breaking left-to-right putt for a round of par 72 and a one-shot victory.

1975: Carnoustie, Scotland

Of the five British Opens contested at Carnoustie only the final one resulted in a tie, that between American Tom Watson and Australian Jack Newton.

Carnoustie lies almost directly across the Firth of Tay from St. Andrews. As expected of a seaside links course, it is relatively flat and always at the mercy of the elements. Because of its many nuances and the length of its holes, many consider it the toughest course in all of Britain. The climax of the course comes at the final three holes. The 235-yard, par-three sixteenth often requires a driver to reach the green. The final two holes, the 454-yard seventeenth and the 448-yard eighteenth, are intersected by the Barry Burn, which snakes its way back and forth across the two fairways.

The Old Course has been the site of four British Open playoffs. Here Jack Nicklaus plays from the fairway of the second hole.

In the final eighteen holes of the 1975 tournament, Watson came from five shots back to gain a tie, shooting 72 for a 279 total, despite three consecutive three-putt greens. Watson was also aided by Newton's collapse when the Aussie blew a two-shot lead with four to play.

The eighteen hole playoff on the following day was decided on two key holes that provided momentum for Watson. The first occurred on the 175-yard, par-three eighth. With the match dead even, Watson pull-hooked a five iron that stayed in bounds by the narrowest of margins. After a pitch to ten feet, Watson made par to Newton's birdie, keeping his deficit at one. The second critical turning point took place at the thirteenth where Watson pitched in for an eagle.

Yet, despite Watson's heroics, they were still even coming to the 448-yard, par-four eighteenth. Playing into a head wind, Watson reached the green in two with a driver and a two iron, while Newton was bunkered in the front. After Newton blasted to twelve feet, Watson putted to three feet and elected to finish, making his par. Newton's tying putt skidded over the left edge of the hole and the victory was Watson's, 71 to 72.

Watson's victory marked his emergence as the dominant player of the time in the Open. Over the next nine years he would win the title five times, the most memorable being his historic duel with Jack Nicklaus at Turnberry in 1977.

For Newton, a young player with a blossoming career, it would be his one and only shining moment. In 1983 he was the victim of a tragic accident in which he lost his right arm and the sight of his right eye when struck by the propeller of an airplane at Sydney's Mascot Airport. Nevertheless, he still continues to play golf today.

1989: Royal Troon, Scotland

The 118th British Open, the sixth conducted over the links of Troon, featured a number of initial experiences for the game's oldest open tournament.

The 1989 championship marked the first occurrence of a three-way tie at the end of regulation play for the championship title. All of the previous twelve playoffs in the Open had involved only two players. But, given the size of the field at the start, 156 players, it was almost inevitable.

The three playoff combatants, Greg Norman and Wayne Grady of Australia and Mark Calcavecchia of the United States, presented a microcosm of the state of the game in the world in 1989. On a globe made smaller by the advance of technology, golf during the 1980s had become an international sport. No longer was it strictly the domain of the Americans. Golf had become such a universal game that non–American players had captured eleven of the major championships contested in the 1980s and seven of the last twenty in the decade.

Secondly, the playoff featured the occurrence of a new format, a four hole aggregate competition. This was the initial test for the format in any major championship. While the concept had been in place since 1984, no Open championship had resulted in a tie since then, affording the opportunity to assay the new design. In the final analysis, the format proved to be both exciting for the fans and fair for the competitors.

So new and innovative was the design of the playoff that Calcavecchia was unaware of the format until moments before the playoff began. He was under the impression that the title would be decided in a sudden-death format.

Finally, this was the first playoff to take place at Troon, located on the west coast of Scotland, and laid out against the Firth of Clyde. Troon, which was originally constructed as a five hole layout in 1878, is at its best when then usual Scottish breeze blows over its links. Unfortunately, the summer of 1989 had been calm and the course was reduced to tabbycat status for the greatest players in the world.

With the country in the midst of a devastating drought, the usual thick and unrelenting rough was virtually nonexistent and the course was playing hard and fast in perfect golfing weather – a condition seldom experienced on the coast of Scotland. While the usual unpredictable bounces remained intact, a shot finding the rough went scarcely unpunished.

With the docile Troon links at the mercy of the best players in the world, rounds in the 60s were more common than the traditional Scottish weather. The thirteen under par total of 275 that produced the playoff tied the record for most strokes under par in the history of the British Open, a mark set at Muirfield in 1980. Twice the course record was broken, once by American Payne Stewart with a second round 65, and again on the final day by Norman with a spectacular 64.

But it was not only the new and unusual playoff format that provided the dramatics for the tournament. The final eighteen holes also featured stellar golf, sprinkled with miraculous shots.

Norman's record-breaking 64 was by far the most spectacular. Beginning the final round seven shots behind third round leader Grady, Norman started his round with six straight birdies to jump into contention just as the leaders were beginning play. After a bogie four at the par-three eighth, the famed "Postage Stamp," Norman made the turn in 31. Coming home he birdied eleven, twelve, and sixteen, and retired to the clubhouse at thirteen under par to wait.

Playing two groups in front of Grady, Calcavecchia started his final round three shots behind and lost ground almost immediately, depsite birdies on the second and fourth. A bogie at number seven left him five shots behind as he made the turn.

Then came the miracles—lucky shots aided by skill that more often than not propel a player to victory in a major championship. On the par-five eleventh Calcavecchia tangled with a thorn bush after his second shot and finally reached the green in four. Left with a forty-footer to save par, he holed it.

But if number eleven was at all skilled for Calcavecchia, then the twelfth was surely supernatural. Lying two on the par four, some fifty yards to the left of the green and with the ball sitting in a small hole, he lofted a wedge toward the flag. The ball struck the flag stick about two feet above the hole and went straight down into the cup for a birdie to put him eleven under.

His birdies on the par five sixteenth and the par-four eighteenth were less spectacular, yet still dramatic and much needed to tie Norman.

Still, it looked like the heroics of Norman and Calcavecchia would all go for naught. Grady began his day with birdies on three of the first five holes to go to fifteen under. He lost a stroke at the ninth with a bogie but regained it with a birdie at twelve. A bogie at the par-three fourteenth reduced his lead to one and he finally fell into a tie with a bogie at another par three, the seventeenth. A par on the last ensured the first three-way playoff in the Open.

One other player remained in contention for most of the day, Tom Watson, whose quest for a record-tying sixth British Open fell short once again. Watson began the day just one shot behind Grady, but the fast birdie pace was too much for Watson's putter, once his most formidable weapon. He finished at eleven under, alone in fourth position.

Under the new and unique playoff format, the four deciding holes included numbers one, two, seventeen, and eighteen, two par fours, a par three, and a par four.

Norman's momentum carried into the playoff as he quickly birdied the first while Grady and Calcavecchia made routine pars. At the second Norman again birdied and was joined by Calcavecchia with a thirty-five-footer from the fringe. Grady parred.

The par-three seventeenth proved to be the turning point. All three players missed the green with their tee shots. Calcavecchia lagged his fifty-footer from the fringe of the green just over the edge of the hole and tapped it in for par. Norman made bogie from the back edge of the green after his chip shot skidded ten feet past and he failed to convert the putt. Grady made bogie from the same bunker he had played out of just a short time earlier and effectively ended his chances for victory.

Now tied with Norman at one under with one hole to play, Calcavecchia hit his drive on the final hole down the right side of the fairway. With the adrenalin pumping, Norman unleashed a mighty blow and flew his drive over three hundred yards, the ball coming to rest in one of those small, devilish Scottish bunkers that most observers thought was unreachable on the drive, despite the hard and fast conditions. Still over two hundred yards away and unaware of Norman's impossible lie in the bunker, Calcavecchia hit a courageous, do-or-die four iron that settled just seven feet from the hole.

Faced with the impossible, Norman could only advance the ball about one hundred yards. The ball finished in another bunker. In a final attempt to salvage par, he slashed the ball over the green and out of bounds.

For the record, Calcavecchia made his birdie to finish two under for the playoff with a total of thirteen strokes.

With his victory Calcavecchia became the first U.S. player to capture the Open since Tom Watson's triumph in 1983. His first victory in a major championship was one that had been expected for some time. Yet this victory was also somewhat aided by Mother Nature. With his wife expecting their first child at any time, Calcavecchia was prepared to withdraw from the tournament at any moment should his wife give birth. Fortunately, she waited. Two weeks later they named their baby Brittany in honor of the Open win.

For Norman, this playoff defeat was another bitter disappointment and lost opportunity in a major championship. It was his third playoff loss in a major championship in the 1980s, tying a mark set by Craig Wood in the 1930s. His loss also marked him as the only player to suffer defeat in three different playoff formats. In 1984 he lost an eighteen hole playoff to Fuzzy Zoeller for the U.S. Open Championship, in 1987 he lost to Larry Mize in a sudden-death playoff in the Masters, and now he had lost in a four hole aggregate playoff.

3
U.S. Open

The United States Golf Association, established December 22, 1884, is responsible for conducting the U.S. Open. The USGA had a controversial beginning — at the center of which was Charles Blair Macdonald, an excellent player and a masterful course architect. Macdonald, however, was a slicer and his many course designs reflected that shot-making deficiency. They were laid out clockwise around the club's property.

In 1894 Macdonald, considered the best golfer in the United States at the time, lost both a stroke play and a match play tournament. He quickly dismissed either as a national championship, claiming that neither was conducted for the sole purpose of determining a national champion.

The problem came into the open. There was a definite need for a national organization to conduct a national championship.

Thus the USGA was born and in October 1895 conducted a national match play championship in Newport, Rhode Island. The tournament had been originally scheduled for September, but was deferred one month, giving way to the America's Cup sailing races also held in Newport.

As a supplement, the newly formed USGA also conducted an "open" championship, a competition for all amateurs as well as the many Scottish and English professionals now serving at clubs in the United States.

The first winner was an Englishman, Horace Rawlins, whose thirty-six hole score tallied 91–82 — 173. In 1898 the U.S. Open expanded to seventy-two holes, following in the footsteps of the British Open which converted to seventy-two holes for 1892 championship. The event was held at the Myopia Hunt Club in South Hamilton, Massachusetts, and required eight trips around the nine hole course in two days.

The first playoff for a U.S. Open championship also occurred at the Myopia Hunt Club in 1901. Including that championship, twenty-nine playoffs have been required to determine the winner.

The U.S. Open has a peculiar history regarding the length of its playoffs. With the inaugural U.S. Open in 1895 at Newport, the scheduled format called for an eighteen hole playoff the following day. In 1928 the playoff length was escalated to thirty-six holes. This led to a marathon 144 hole championship (seventy-two holes of regulation play, seventy-two holes of playoff) between Billy Burke and George Von Elm in 1931. The next year the U.S. Open returned to the eighteen hole format for all playoffs. Today it remains the only major championship that preserves the eighteen hole playoff to resolve ties for the title. The only concession being that if the playoff results in a tie, a sudden-death will then determine the winner.

1901: Myopia Hunt Club, Hamilton, Massachusetts

Willie Anderson, representing the Pittsfield (Mass.) Country Club, defeated Alex Smith 84 to 85 in the eighteen hole playoff, the first in U.S. Open history, after the pair had tied at the end of seventy-two holes with 331, the highest winning score ever recorded for a U.S. Open. For Anderson it was the first of four U.S. Open victories in the span of five years that included three consecutive wins from 1903–5.

Anderson was the typical Scot, always businesslike and never smiling. He was a gruff, hard-drinking man who died at the age of thirty from hardening of the arteries, probably a result of his fondness for whiskey.

In contrast, Alex Smith was just the opposite, always smiling and friendly with a hearty sense of humor.

The tournament was characterized by hard ground, thin grass, thick rough, and lightning fast greens which made even the shortest putt treacherous. It was reported that one competitor "charged" a downhill putt at the eighth and watched as his ball rolled off the green and into the shrubs. From the concern for equipment, this was the last U.S. Open played with the gutta-percha ball.

While regulation play in the championship ended on a Friday, the required playoff had to be postponed until Monday as the course was reserved for members on weekends.

1903: Baltusrol Golf Course, Springfield, New Jersey

Willie Anderson, now representing the Apawamis Club in Rye, New York, but formerly of the Baltusrol Club, made his homecoming a memorable one by winning his second U.S. Open title in the second playoff for the championship. This time he defeated David Brown, winner of the 1886 British Open, 82 to 84 after both had finished with seventy-two hole scores of 307.

With his victory Anderson became the first man to win the U.S. Open title twice. This was also the second Open in which players used the Haskell ball, the forerunner of today's golf ball. With that ball Anderson produced a record score of 73 in the first round.

1908: Myopia Hunt Club, Hamilton, Massachusetts

In 1908 the U.S. Open visited the Myopia Hunt Club for the fourth and final time. The course was still enjoying its status as one of the premier layouts in the country. It was the brainchild of Herbert C. Leeds, a first-rate player who took it upon himself to improve the lot of golf course architecture around the turn of the century. While he designed other courses — most notably the Palmetto Country Club in Aiken, South Carolina — he remained at Myopia for most of his life, constantly fine-tuning the course.

In an eighteen hole playoff Fred McLeod, a Scot playing out of the Midlothian Country Club in Chicago, defeated Willie Smith 77 to 83 after a seventy-two hole tie at 322.

To this day, McLeod remains the smallest man to win the U.S. Open. A diminutive five feet five inches, McLeod began the tournament weighing 118 pounds and finished at just 108 pounds.

1910: Philadelphia Cricket Club, Philadelphia, Pennsylvania

Alex "miss 'em quick" Smith missed an easy three-foot putt on the seventy-second hole that would have given him the championship outright. But Smith, who possessed a remarkably relaxed attitude toward the game, quite simply shook it off.

However, it should be mentioned that he did have some assistance from the law in forgetting his blunder. Although the tournament ended on Saturday, the playoff was conducted on Monday, abiding by the law that no competitive golf was permitted on Sunday. Nevertheless, he won handily in the Monday playoff, shooting 71 to defeat eighteen-year-old Johnny McDermott (75) and his twenty-year-old brother McDonald Smith (77).

1911: Chicago Golf Club, Wheaton, Illinois

Johnny McDermott (80) won a three-way playoff over Mike Brady (82) and George Simpson (85) at the Chicago Golf Club in Wheaton, Illinois.

The Chicago Golf Club has a valued history in the annals of American golf. Originally designed by Charles Blair Macdonald, it was one of five charter members of the USGA and was the site of many early national championships, including three U.S. Opens and four U.S. Amateurs.

The playoff had a curious beginning when McDermott succumbed to the desires of money. Normally playing a Rawlings Black Circle ball, McDermott accepted the offer of a manufacturer who promised a $300 bonus to the playoff winner if he used a brand called Colonel. McDermott promptly hit two balls out of bounds from the first tee, but luckily escaped with a six owing to the fact that there was but a one-stroke penalty for out of bounds in that day. So much for the Colonel.

Johnny McDermott, who represented the Atlantic City Country Club, was 130 pounds of cocksure golfer who learned the game in the caddy yards of Philadelphia. At nineteen years ten months he was the youngest Open winner, and his victory generated previously unseen interest in the tournament.

Tragically, his success was short lived. His sudden and meteoric rise to the top of the golfing world had a decided effect on his nerves. Although he enjoyed more success in 1914 when he won the North and South Open, his nerves soon gave out and he suffered a mental breakdown and disappeared from competitive golf. He died at the age of 80 in 1971.

With the 1911 U.S. Open the balance of power in the world of golf began to shift. McDermott became the first homebred boy to win the U.S. Open title and his victory signaled the end of the British reign in the U.S. Open. A true-blooded American, one born and raised in the United States, had finally won the U.S. Open. But the final blow was still to come.

1913: The Country Club, Brookline, Massachusetts

September 20, 1913. Even the exact date of twenty-year-old Francis Ouimet's playoff victory over the British giants Harry Vardon and Ted Ray is worth remembering for it marks the precise turning point in U.S. golf.

While Ouimet was not the first homebred American to win the championship — that distinction went to Johnny McDermott in 1911 — he was the first amateur to capture the title at a time when championships of this sort were totally dominated by professionals.

Ouimet's victory contains all of the elements necessary to make a playoff historically significant.

The playoff involved two of the established stars of the game at that time, the great Harry Vardon and his colleague Ted Ray. These two British gentlemen were the pinnacle of golf. Vardon had already captured one U.S. Open and five of his eventual six British Opens. Ray had won the 1912 British Open and would go on to win the 1920 U.S. Open.

To say that Ouimet was the definitive underdog is most certainly a decided understatement. He was, in essence, the ultimate David facing off against the game's two Goliaths. Vardon and Ray were already legendary heroes of the game both in Great Britain and the United States.

Prior to Ouimet's stunning victory, golf was essentially back-page filler material for the press. His victory instantly elevated golf to the top of the American sporting life. U.S. golfers had for several years been on the verge of a major emergence as far as the quality of their play was concerned. Johnny McDermott's U.S. Open victories in 1911 and 1912 had signaled that emergence.

Ouimet provided volumes of human interest for the media. Golf was not his profession. He was a sporting goods salesman for Wright and Ditson. He was self-taught, learning the game in a field behind his home, adjacent to The Country Club, with old, discarded clubs and lost and found golf balls.

Most importantly, Ouimet was the epitome of a gentleman. While the story of the golfer is great, the tale of the man is even greater. In the years following his stunning victory, he never permitted his sudden success to swell his pride. He never aspired to gain wealth from his victory. He shunned professional golf as a career, preferring to play the game as an amateur. In the year following his U.S. Open victory, he captured the French and U.S. Amateurs, considered at that time more prestigious events than the U.S. Open. America could not have asked for a more worthy, humble champion.

Ironically, Ouimet initially declined to compete in the tournament because of his job. He felt he had already taken enough time off to play golf that season, a season that included winning the Massachusetts Amateur and a semifinal loss to Jerry Travers in the U.S. Amateur. Even after being coaxed by the president of the USGA to enter, Ouimet still resisted. He had exhausted his vacation time from his job. Fortunately, his boss insisted that he should play.

Ouimet's moment has been described in many terms by the golfing press: "The Shots Heard 'Round the World"; "David versus Goliath"; and "The Ultimate Cinderella Story." But, whatever you choose to label it, the impact on the American golf scene cannot be diminished.

Ouimet provided the dramatics in regulation play as well. Despite being deadlocked with Vardon and Ray at the end of fifty-four holes, Ouimet was not expected to contend. There would most certainly be too much pressure on the young amateur. And when he toured the front nine of the final round in 43 and began the back nine with a bogie at the tenth, everyone conceded that he had put up a good fight, but the battle was lost.

But for Ouimet the challenge had just begun. Even after he

bogied the twelfth he did not consider himself out of the race.
Knowing that he needed two birdies and four pars in the final six
holes to tie Vardon and Ray who finished at 304, Ouimet carefully
calculated his strategy. He figured his best birdie chances would
come on the thirteenth, a short par four, and the sixteenth, a relatively easy par three.

After a birdie on the thirteenth, thanks to a chip-in, and a par
on fourteen, he saved par on the fifteenth after a poor approach.
Next was the sixteenth, his other projected birdie hole. He played
the hole poorly and ultimately had to sink a nine-foot putt to save
par. Now he needed a birdie on seventeen or eighteen to tie. The
seventeenth was a dogleg left par four. He played two shots to
twenty feet, but his putt was not easy. Downhill and sidehill. His
stroke was a bit too firm but the ball hit the hole dead center and
dropped in.

Now a par on eighteen would give him a tie. A drive in the fairway, his second just short of the green, a chip to five feet, and a
smooth, nerveless putt preserved the tie. Ouimet was carried off
the green by the gallery.

One interested spectator in Ouimet's gallery over the final
holes had been Vardon who years later in *My Golfing Life* freely
admitted that, after watching Ouimet play the final four holes in
one under par, it was one of the most courageous displays of golf
he had ever witnessed in a national championship.

With Ouimet's courageous golf to gain a tie, history had been
made. But chapter two was yet to come.

The eighteen hole playoff came the next morning under wet
and miserable conditions. Ouimet awoke at 8 A.M. and ate break-
fast at home. The walk to the club was one he had made many
times before, only this time it was not to sneak in a few holes before
the greenskeeper arrived.

Unquestionably, it is the most historic round of golf ever
played. There have been other great rounds—Jones at Sunningdale, Venturi at Congressional, Nicklaus at Augusta—but
none have affected the game of golf in the manner this one did.

A stroke by stroke account would be appropriate, but cumber-
some and not fitting to this account. In brief, after the first nine all
three were tied at 38, despite some tense, up and down golf.
Ouimet went ahead for the first time on the tenth when both Vardon and Ray three-putted and he parred. He picked up another
stoke on the twelfth with a par, but Vardon got a stroke back on

the thirteenth with a birdie. All made loose but regulation pars on the fourteenth.

On the fifteenth Ray, who had been spraying the ball all day, faltered with a double-bogie six and all but fell out of contention. Vardon and Ouimet made par. But the pressure had begun to show on Vardon also. No one could ever remember Vardon lighting a cigarette on the golf course. But with the pressure mounting, he did on the fifteenth.

Vardon and Ouimet both made par on the sixteenth. Then, still having the honor but also trailing by a shot, Vardon gambled on the seventeenth. The gamble failed. He hit into the bunker at the corner of the dogleg. The best he could make was a bogie five.

Meanwhile, Ouimet had played the hole much like the day before, two shots on the green eighteen feet away. A two putt and he would carry a two-shot lead to the final hole. Instead, he holed it for a birdie and a three-shot lead with one to play.

He played the last in regulation, two on and two putts. It was over, golf in the United States was changed forever.

For the record the final was Ouimet 72, Vardon 77, and Ray 78.

Ouimet's concentration in the playoff was almost supernatural. Being the hometown boy and now national hero, he was constantly besieged by friends and wellwishers, between shots and between green and tee. Just how he maintained his even nerve was simply miraculous.

Ouimet's impact on the American golf scene was almost immediate. Records indicate that the day he won the Open there were 350,000 golfers in the United States. Ten years later there were 2 million.

1919: Brae Burn Country Club, Boston, Massachusetts

The annals of golf are filled with legendary heroes from Old Tom Morris to Jack Nicklaus, but none is more colorful than Walter Hagen. Affectionately known as "the Haig," he captured the 1919 U.S. Open in a playoff over one of the most tragic figures in U.S. Open history, Mike Brady. This was Hagen's second U.S. Open triumph and curiously his last, despite his dominance of

Macdonald Smith, Bing Crosby, and Walter Hagen. Smith lost the 1910 playoff for the U.S. Open to his brother Alex. Hagen captured the 1919 U.S. Open with a playoff victory over Mike Brady.

professional golf throughout the 1920s. For Brady it was his second playoff loss in the championship.

Hagen was the son of a blacksmith in Rochester, New York. He effectively dropped out of school at age twelve. By fifteen he was the assistant pro at the Country Club of Rochester and at nineteen became head professional. An accomplished baseball player, he was once offered a tryout with the Philadelphia Phillies by manager Pat Moran.

Hagen is singularly responsible for the reformation of the image of the golf professional. At the time of Hagen's rise, golf professionals were considered second-class citizens at the golf course. More often than not, they were not even permitted in the clubhouse. But Hagen changed all that. With his flair for the dramatic and his colorful personality, he elevated the position of golf professional to the top of the athletic ladder.

As a consequence of World War I, this was the first Open played since 1916. The victory solidified Hagen as one of the leading professionals of the day, British or American.

In his final six holes of regulation play Hagen was one under fours which gained him a tie with Brady. In typical Hagen style he came to the seventy-second hole needing a ten-foot birdie putt to win the championship. Seizing the moment as he always did, he brashly called for Brady, who had stumbled in earlier with an 80, to come to the green and watch. His putt hit the edge of the hole and spun out.

The playoff, of course, had a bit of the Hagen colorfulness included. Coming to the seventeenth, Hagen held a two-shot advantage. After a wild drive, it was Brady who found Hagen's ball embedded in mud. Hagen claimed a spectator must have stepped on the ball, but that thought was quickly discarded by tournament officials. However, they could not deny his request to identify his ball. After cleaning and identifying his ball, Hagen replaced it with the touch of a surgeon. The ball stayed above ground and Hagen salvaged a five out of what could easily have been six or seven to Brady's four. He won by a stroke, 77 to 78.

1923: Inwood Country Club, Long Island, New York

Bobby Jones, whose frustration in the Open had grown year by year, particularly in 1922 when he finished a stroke behind Gene Sarazen, finally captured his first of four U.S. Open championships.

His play over the final holes of regulation was indicative of that frustration. Coming to the seventy-second hole, Jones was reeling. He had just bogied sixteen and seventeen and desperately needed a par to put away the championship. His frustration was magnified in his loose play. He staggered to a double-bogie six after dumping a pitch shot into a greenside bunker.

Likewise, Bobby Cruickshank, a diminutive Scot with a big heart who had been a prisoner of war in World War I, had ample opportunity to win. But he too gave away strokes coming in with a double-bogie on sixteen and needed a birdie on eighteen to tie Jones. He rose to the occasion by playing a magnificent final hole with a drive, mid-iron, and six-foot putt.

The playoff was an up and down affair with only two of the first seventeen holes being tied. Cruickshank birdied three of the first five for a two-shot lead. But by the thirteenth, Jones had

fought back and held a two-shot advantage. Cruickshank struck back and regained the strokes on the fourteenth and fifteenth. Jones went ahead again at sixteen but Cruickshank evened the match at the seventeenth.

They stood on the eighteenth tee of the playoff all even. Cruickshank drove poorly into a stiff breeze, hitting a weak hook to the left and was forced to lay up short of a lake guarding the green. Jones's drive had drifted off the fairway to the right and set-tled on bare dirt. Then, executing one of the most courageous shots in golf, Jones hit a 200-yard two iron over the lagoon six feet from the hole. The best Cruickshank could do was six against Jones's four. Jones had finally won a national championship, 76 to 78.

The victory officially ushered in the Bobby Jones era. Over the next seven years Jones would win twelve more major champion-ships and totally dominate the world of golf in a manner in which no other player ever has, before or since.

1925: Worcester Country Club, Worcester, Massachusetts

Bobby Jones's quest for a second U.S. Open was frustrated when he lost in a playoff to Willie Macfarlane, a club pro who sel-dom played tournament golf. Both Jones and Macfarlane, along with eight or ten others, including Hagen, Ouimet, and Sarazen, had a chance to win in regulation play. In fact, the competition was so close that with one hole to play seven men still had the chance to win. But in the end only Jones and Macfarlane survived at 291.

They parlayed the customary eighteen hole playoff into a thirty-six hole affair, when the first eighteen holes resulted in a tie at 75 with neither player taking more than a one-shot lead. And when Macfarlane missed a six-footer on the last hole to secure a victory, Jones made a five-foot sidehiller to tie and force a second eighteen hole playoff. This was the first double round playoff in Open history.

On the second eighteen holes, which were played in the after-noon, Jones led by four shots after nine holes and his second Open

Opposite: The 18th hole at Inwood Country Club where in 1923 Bobby Jones defeated "Wee" Bobby Cruickshank in a playoff for the U.S. Open Championship.

victory seemed assured. Surely no one could make up four strokes on Bobby Jones in nine holes? But coming home Jones played raggedly, shooting 38 for a 73, while Macfarlane was brilliant with a 33, including two twos, for a 72 and a one-shot victory.

Jones's loss only added to a long and growing list of could have beens and should have beens in the U.S. Open.

1927: Oakmont Country Club, Oakmont, Pennsylvania

On one of the most difficult and demanding courses ever played in the U.S. Open, Tommy Armour, a transplanted Scottish professional, defeated Harry Cooper, a twenty-three-year-old ex-Englishman, in an eighteen hole playoff, 76 to 79.

In regulation play Armour played the last six holes two under par including a ten-foot birdie on the final hole to tie Cooper at 301 who himself had three-putted the seventy-second green.

Armour, who hailed from Edinburgh, Scotland, is a story of great courage. After losing the sight of one eye during World War I, he again resumed his amateur career and in 1921 was selected to the British team to compete against the United States in the forerunner to the Walker Cup. Three years later he turned professional and by 1931 had won all three of the major professional championships.

Armour also became known as a master teacher of the game and was sought after by players of all calibers. His book, *How to Play Your Best Golf All the Time* has become a classic of golf instruction.

1928: Olympia Fields Country Club, Chicago, Illinois

Early in 1928 the USGA resolved that any ties for the championship would be decided by a thirty-six hole playoff, a length that they felt was much more suitable to determine a national champion. And, as fate would have it, for the second consecutive year the U.S. Open went to a playoff. Bobby Jones and Johnny Farrell tied at 294.

Be that as it may, the playoff should never have taken place. Roland Hancock, an unheralded twenty-one-year-old professional from North Carolina, needed only a pair of fives on the last two holes to win the championship. But, the pressure was too much and he succumbed. He made six on each of the holes and finished one stroke behind Jones and Farrell.

In the playoff Farrell finished the first eighteen holes with four consecutive birdies to take a three-stroke lead, 70 to 73. But in the afternoon, Farrell faded badly and the players were all even with three to go. A bogie by Jones on the sixteenth (the thirty-fourth of the playoff) gave Farrell a one-shot lead and both birdied seventeen, with Jones holing a thirty-footer after Farrell lay two feet for a birdie.

On the last hole Farrell tried to nurse his one-stroke lead and, as is often the case, played feebly, lying two, fifty yards short of the green on the par five. Jones played two steady shots and was on in two and another playoff looked imminent. Farrell pitched to eight feet and Jones two-putted. But with the pressure at its utmost, Farrell seized the moment and holed his putt for a one-shot victory.

For Jones this had been his third playoff in the U.S. Open in six years and his second loss. However, he had not lost to a virtual unknown. Farrell was one of the top professionals of the day. In the previous five Opens he had finished no worse than seventh, with his best showing being one stroke behind Jones and Macfarlane in 1925. Nevertheless, it would be Farrell's only Open triumph.

1929: Winged Foot Golf Club, Mamaroneck, New York

In 1929 there was a third straight playoff in the U.S. Open and the fourth for Bobby Jones since 1923. His opponent this time was Al Espinosa, a World War I veteran of Spanish descent.

However, it was not the playoff that provided the excitement, but rather the final hole of regulation play. It is the stuff from which the Bobby Jones legend grew and continues today.

Coming to the final hole and needing a par four to tie, Jones pulled his approach to the left of the green. With the ball sitting well below his feet, Jones pitched to twelve feet and then holed the sharply breaking, left-to-right putt.

The thirty-six hole playoff was anticlimactic. Espinosa was no match for Jones. In the most lopsided playoff in major championship history Jones scored 72–69 – 141 to Espinosa's 84–80 – 164 and won by twenty-three strokes.

1931: Inverness Club, Toledo, Ohio

Aside from the fact that this was the first U.S. Open in which the winner played with steel shafted clubs, the championship was a milestone in two respects. It was the first Open held after the retirement of Bobby Jones. The tournament field was wide open. For the first time in over five years there was no definitive favorite to whom the fans could cling.

Second, it featured the longest playoff in golf history, seventy-two holes. The USGA was still resolving all ties for the championship with a thirty-six hole playoff, a practice initiated in 1928. Unfortunately, in 1931 the first thirty-six hole playoff ended in a tie, requiring a second thirty-six holes to determine the winner.

The marathon battle was waged between Billy Burke, a little known professional from Connecticut, and George Von Elm, the 1926 U.S. Amateur Champion, who had defeated Bobby Jones in the final of that event. Both tied at the end of seventy-two holes with 292.

Over the first eighteen holes of the playoff Burke shot 73 to Vol Elm's 75. But when Burke shot 40 on the outward nine of the afternoon, Von Elm jumped ahead by two with nine to play. Unable to hold the lead, Von Elm had to birdie the final hole to force a second thirty-six holes the next day.

The second thirty-six holes nearly resulted in another tie. With five holes to play the match was still all even. Finally Burke gained a stroke and when Von Elm failed to birdie the eighteenth for the tie, Burke had won. Over the second thirty-six holes he shot 77–71 – 148 to Von Elm's 76–73 – 149 for a slender, one-stroke victory after the pair had played 144 holes.

With a playoff that nearly went to fifty-four holes, the thirty-six hole playoff format finally met a timely, albeit belated, demise. The following year the USGA returned to eighteen holes to settle all ties, exactly where it remains today.

Jock Hutchison, a victor in the 1921 playoff for the British Open; Fred McLeod, winner of the U.S. Open playoff in 1908; Nevin Gibson, picture provider for this volume; and Billy Burke, winner of the longest playoff in history—144 holes in the 1931 U.S. Open.

1939: Philadelphia Country Club, Philadelphia, Pennsylvania

Despite the three-way playoff among Byron Nelson, Craig Wood, and Denny Shute, the first since the Ouimet-Vardon-Ray battle in 1913, the 1939 U.S. Open will always be remembered for Sam Snead's catastrophic triple-bogie eight on the seventy-second hole. Snead came to the hole needing only a five to better by two shots the 284 totals of Nelson, Wood, and Shute. A par five on the 555-yard hole would have given him the championship outright.

But pressure affects everyone, including the seasoned professional. After a poor drive in the left rough, Snead tried to gain maximum distance on his second and scraped the ball into a fairway bunker about 100 yards from the green. After failing to escape on his first attempt, Snead staggered to an eight on the hole and squandered all hopes of winning. The triple bogie did not even qualify Snead for the playoff. Whether or not this collapse had any bearing on his future Open exploits is difficult to determine. From

Craig Wood: A most tragic figure in the history of playoffs. From 1933 to 1939 Wood lost three consecutive playoffs in major championships— the 1933 British Open, the 1935 Masters, and the 1939 U.S. Open.

this point on, Snead was snakebit in the Open. Sadly, he was never to win the U.S. Open.

Wood provided the dramatics in regulation play with a birdie on the seventy-second after hitting the green in two to get into the playoff. Shute had an opportunity to win the tournament outright with pars on the final two holes but bogied the seventeenth to fall into the playoff.

In the playoff on the following day Shute was never a factor and faltered home with a 76. Wood and Nelson meanwhile played head to head for the entire round, never more than a stroke apart. When Nelson three-putted the seventeenth and Wood birdied, Wood held a one-stroke lead and had the Open in hand with only the par-five eighteenth remaining. But Nelson birdied and Wood missed a four-foot, winning putt to send the tournament to another eighteen holes the following day.

Nelson took command of the second eighteen holes with a birdie three on the third and an eagle two on the fourth where he holed his one iron second shot. He finished the round with 70, three strokes in front of Wood for his first U.S. Open victory.

While Wood was considered an all-around shot maker and won the Masters and the U.S. Open in 1941, he was a most tragic character in the annals of playoffs. During a seven-year stretch from 1933–39 there were three playoffs for major championships. Wood was a participant and a loser in all three. He and Greg Norman are the only players to be involved in more than two championship playoffs and never win.

1940: Canterbury Golf Club, Cleveland, Ohio

The 1940 U.S. Open will always have the scar of Ed "Porky" Oliver overshadowing the last, great competitive run of Gene Sarazen. The seventy-two hole championship proper ended in a tie at 287 between thirty-eight-year-old Gene Sarazen and Lawson Little, the winner of the 1934 and 1935 U.S. and British Amateur championships who was now a professional.

Oliver also had returned a score of 287 that would have tied him with Little and Sarazen. But Oliver was one of six players who were disqualified for starting ahead of their official starting times.

Lawson Little won his U.S. Open championship in 1940 with a playoff victory over Gene Sarazen.

In a hasty effort to beat an impending storm, all six had started their rounds in the absence of the official starter Joe Dey of the USGA who was in the clubhouse having lunch.

Epitomizing the true sportsmanship of the game, Sarazen and Little determined between them to have Oliver included in the playoff. But the USGA stood firm; Oliver was disqualified.

Oliver's misfortune completely obscured a remarkable back nine performance by Sarazen. Needing a 34 on the final nine to tie for the championship, Sarazen reached back one more time to perform a miracle. After making birdies on the eleventh and thirteenth, he holed critical putts for par on the sixteenth and seventeenth to tie.

Unfortunately, Sarazen was unable to maintain the pace in the resulting playoff and Little, playing steady golf, won 70 to 73.

1946: Canterbury Golf Club, Cleveland, Ohio

The 1946 U.S. Open was the first held after its suspension 1942–45 due to World War II. Fittingly, the last previous tie had been at Canterbury in 1940.

The regulation seventy-two holes ended in a three-way tie among Lloyd Mangrum, Byron Nelson, and Vic Ghezzi. Ben Hogan could have made it a foursome in the playoff, but in an attempt to win the tournament outright on the seventy-second green, he boldly charged a downhill birdie putt and then missed the five-foot return. Nelson might also have won the tournament in regulation were he not victimized by his caddie who accidently stepped on his ball after pushing his way through the unruly crowds. The penalty: one stroke.

In the playoff Lloyd Mangrum, a decorated World War II hero, had to endure through two eighteen-hole rounds in defeating Nelson and Ghezzi. Over the first eighteen holes the three were virtually deadlocked the entire way. All shot even par 72 and forced an afternoon round.

In the afternoon round Mangrum trailed both Nelson and Ghezzi by two at the turn, but birdied fifteen and sixteen to take a two-shot lead. At this point a thunderstorm hit but the threesome played on. Both Mangrum and Nelson bogied seventeen, and when Ghezzi left a four-foot par putt short on the eighteenth, Mangrum was the champion.

Not only was Mangrum one of the best professionals of his day, he was also a supreme patriot. When World War II broke out, he answered the call of his country. For his heroics in combat, he was awarded two Purple Hearts. When the war was over, he resumed his professional career eventually collecting thirty-six tournament victories. He died in 1973 at the age of fifty-nine.

Burned out from the grind of competitive golf, this was Nelson's last U.S. Open. He virtually retired from competitive golf at age thirty-four.

1947: St. Louis Country Club, St. Louis, Missouri

While the role of gamesmanship in golf is usually downplayed and is most always subtle, the playoff for the 1947 U.S. Open championship featured one of the most overt cases on record. It also helped to perpetuate Sam Snead's jinx in the Open.

In regulation play Lou Worsham was in the clubhouse with a score of 282. Snead, who had just bogied the seventeenth, stood on the seventy-second tee needing a birdie to tie for the championship. Reaching the par-four hole in two, he gallantly sank an eighteen-foot putt to force a playoff. Many thought that his jinx in the Open would come to an end.

And indeed in the playoff on the following day, when Snead was ahead by one after nine and two after fifteen, it did appear that he would finally win the Open. But Worsham birdied the sixteenth and, coupled with a sloppy bogie by Snead at the seventeenth, the two headed to the final hole all even. The stage was set.

On the par-four eighteenth with Snead already on in two, twenty feet away, Worsham hit his second just over the green into the long grass, a trademark at U.S. Open courses. His fine chip skidded just over the edge of the hole and stopped two and one half feet away. Snead putted next and his downhiller stopped about the same distance short of the hole. But just as Snead prepared to putt, Worsham called for a measurement, realizing that the one farther from the hole was entitled to putt first.

The measurement showed that Snead was indeed away, thirty and one-half inches, to Worsham's twenty-nine and one-half. With that brief pause for measurement, Snead had been distracted. He putted first, striking the ball too lightly and missing to the right, the ball not even touching the hole. Worsham sank his straight uphill putt and was the Open champion. Once again Snead had failed to win the Open.

1950: Merion Golf Club, Ardmore, Pennsylvania

In February 1949 Ben Hogan, the 1948 U.S. Open champion, had been involved in a near fatal auto accident in west Texas. With initial predictions stating that he would never play golf again, Hogan returned to the tour at the start of the 1950 season. Forever the master of mind over matter, Hogan competed, despite aching and swollen legs wrapped in elastic bandages. So it was in June 1950, just sixteen months after his accident, that he began competition in the fiftieth U.S. Open.

Ben Hogan, one of the top players of all time. He won only one of four playoffs in which he participated, the 1950 U.S. Open at Merion.

Hogan stayed close to the lead throughout the first two rounds, but with the standard double round scheduled for Saturday, Hogan was understandably unsure how he would endure. This would be his first double round since the accident.

In the morning of the final day he played through to a steady 72 that put him just two shots off the lead, and by the time he had reached the twelfth tee of the final round, his steady golf had built a three-shot lead. But by then the pain in his legs was growing steadily with every step. On the twelfth tee he nearly collapsed hitting his tee shot, but still managed to continue.

From the twelfth through the seventeenth he squandered away the three-stroke margin with bogies on twelve, fifteen, and seventeen. Then on the eighteenth, a testing 458-yard par four he hit one of golf's most memorable shots, a one iron to the left front portion of the green, forty feet from the cup and two-putted. He had tied Lloyd Mangrum and George Fazio at 287, seven over par.

In the playoff on the following day Hogan took an early lead but was caught by Mangrum at the end of nine holes. Fazio was just one shot back. At the end of fifteen holes Hogan had gained a slender one-shot lead over Mangrum while Fazio had faded out of contention.

Controversy came on the par-four sixteenth. Hogan reached the green in regulation but Mangrum was forced to lay up after a poor drive. Mangrum recovered to eight feet. He marked his ball to allow Hogan and Fazio to putt. After they had putted and made their pars, Mangrum replaced his ball. But before putting, in a momentary mental lapse, Mangrum marked his ball a second time, picked it up, and blew off a bug. He replaced the ball and made the putt for par.

Under the rules at that time, a ball could be marked and cleaned only once. It could not be lifted again for any reason.

Before playing off the seventeenth tee, Mangrum was informed of the two-stroke penalty by a USGA official. Mangrum was naturally despondent. He now trailed Hogan by three, vice one, and his chances had slipped away. Hogan then proceeded to birdie the seventeenth with a fifty-foot putt to end all doubt. He finished with a 69 to Mangrum's 73 and Fazio's 75.

The victory solidified Hogan's comeback for the accident and reestablished him as the leading player of the day.

1955: Olympic Country Club, San Francisco, California

Tradition is much like a fine wine. It takes years or even decades to mature. Seldom, if ever, can the process be hurried. Yet the Olympic Club is a rare exception.

The San Francisco Olympic Club contains two courses: the Ocean and the Lake—which is the more challenging of the two and the one used for major championships. The key thought for play on the Lake Course is accuracy. The layout is carved from a forest of pine, eucalyptus, and cypress trees and features narrow, slanting fairways and small, well-trapped greens. Any errant shot is punished severely.

In 1955 the scenic San Francisco layout was host to its first U.S. Open and therein began a history of thwarting the established star's dream of greater glory and elevating the unknown to national champion. It has now become tradition.

Ben Hogan had finished his final round for a seventy-two hole total of 287 as Jack Fleck stood on the tenth tee needing to shoot the final nine in one under 34 to tie Hogan. When Fleck bogied the fourteenth, Hogan appeared to have won his fifth U.S. Open. In the locker room the press began to gather around the soon to be five-time U.S. Open champion.

But, Fleck, a thirty-two-year-old municipal course pro from Davenport, Iowa, wasn't through. He birdied the par-three fifteenth from eight feet and then parred the sixteenth and seventeenth. Still he needed a birdie on the par-four eighteenth to tie. He responded by holing a sliding right-to-left eight-footer. Despite his dramatics, few gave him a chance to win the playoff against Hogan the next day.

In the playoff Fleck, who was supposed to crack under the pressure, surged steadily ahead. He led by two after nine and three after a birdie on ten. Hogan regained a stroke on the eleventh but gave it back on the twelfth. On the fourteenth Hogan again fought back with a par to Fleck's bogie. He picked up another stroke on the seventeenth with a par and as they moved to the eighteenth tee, Fleck's lead had dwindled to just one stroke. But Hogan, feeling he needed a birdie to extend the match further, pressed his drive and the ball hooked into the deep rough on the left. The best he could make was six for a round of 72. Fleck parred for a 69 and the U.S. Open championship.

Jack Fleck performed the seemingly impossible with a playoff victory over Ben Hogan in the 1955 U.S. Open at Olympic.

For Fleck this would be his one illustrious moment in golf. While he did contend briefly on the final day of the 1960 U.S. Open, he faded on the back nine under the drama of the Palmer charge. He finished three shots behind Palmer, tied for third.

But most unfortunately, this tournament in effect marked the end of the Hogan era. While he was still to have moments of brilliance, most notably in the Opens of 1956, 1959, and 1960, he was never to win another major championship.

Opposite: The 18th hole at the Olympic Country Club, San Francisco, California. Two U.S. Open playoffs have occurred there—1955 and 1966.

1957: Inverness Country Club, Toledo, Ohio

It is seldom that a U.S. Open champion is successful in defending his title. Only six have achieved that milestone: Willie Anderson, 1903–5; Johnny McDermott, 1911–12; Bobby Jones, 1929–30; Ralph Guldahl, 1937–38; Ben Hogan, 1950–51; and Curtis Strange, 1988–89.

Even more rare is the case when a defending champion enters a playoff in defense of his title. Such was the circumstance in 1957 when Cary Middlecoff, the 1956 champion, squared off against Dick Mayer in an eighteen hole playoff after the pair had tied at 282.

Middlecoff, forever the nervous and tempestuous sort, began the final day of regulation play eight shots out of the lead shared by Mayer and Billy Joe Patton. Over the last thirty-six holes he shot 68–68, tying a final thirty-six hole record, to gain a playoff with Mayer.

The final hole of regulation play provided one of the most exciting finishes in U.S. Open history. First Mayer, playing about an hour in front of Middlecoff, came to the eighteenth needing a birdie to take the lead from Jimmy Demaret. There was never a doubt over his nine-foot putt. He rapped the ball straight into the hole. Finally Middlecoff came to the eighteenth needing a birdie to tie Mayer. His birdie putt of approximately the same length appeared to die at the hole but fell in at the last instant. Middlecoff still had his chance to become the sixth repeat winner of the Open.

The playoff, however, proved to be anticlimatic. Middlecoff's nerves, which were always taut and on edge, were sprung. He struggled through the playoff with a 79 and lost to Mayer's 72.

1962: Oakmont Country Club, Oakmont, Pennsylvania

Golf, like most other sports, passes through seasons of great players. At times the eras may overlap; in other instances there are periods of years before another great and dominant player comes on the scene.

In the late 1950s and early 1960s Arnold Palmer was unquestionably the dominant player in the game. Palmer had won the U.S. Open in 1960 in most dramatic style, coming from seven shots back with a final round 65 at Cherry Hills, outside Denver. He was the heir to Hogan and those before him. He had become famous for his final round heroics. The galleries adored his aggressive, charging style of play, just as they had Hogan's controlled aggressiveness.

But as Palmer reached his prime in the early 1960s, a young amateur named Jack Nicklaus came on the scene. Winner of the 1959 and 1961 U.S. Amateurs and a runner-up to Palmer at Cherry Hills as an amateur, Nicklaus entered his first full-time season as a professional in 1962.

As fate would have it, Palmer and Nicklaus were paired together in the first two rounds of the 1962 Open. Palmer got the better of the head-to-head duel shooting 71–68 to Nicklaus's 72–70. Palmer's third round 73 kept him two strokes ahead of Nicklaus with just eighteen more to go.

With birdies on two of the first four holes of the final round, Palmer surged four strokes in front of Nicklaus. But then, in what proved to be an omen of future Opens, Palmer lost his entire lead over the next nine holes. With but five holes remaining, they stood all even. When both failed to birdie the short par-four seventeenth, the tournament came down to the seventy-second hole. On the last both missed makable birdie putts, first Nicklaus from twelve feet, then Palmer from ten feet. There would be a playoff the next day.

Palmer fell behind early in the playoff, trailing by four strokes after six holes. Then the famous Palmer charge kicked in. He birdied nine, eleven, and twelve and with six to play was just one stroke behind. But when he three-putted the thirteenth and fell two strokes behind the match was all but over. Nicklaus finished with a 71 to Palmer's 74.

The torch had been passed but Palmer's flame still burned.

1963: The Country Club, Brookline, Massachusetts

For some reason, known only to the gods of gold, certain courses, almost always the great ones, produce the dramatic. In

Julius Boros appeared in one playoff and was victorious over Arnold Palmer and Jacky Cupit in the 1963 U.S. Open at the Country Club in Brookline, Massachusetts.

observance of the fiftieth anniversary of Francis Ouimet's stunning and historical victory in the 1913 U.S. Open, the USGA returned its premier tournament to The Country Club in Brookline, Massachusetts. Once again, The Country Club produced its magic with another three-way playoff to decide the title.

One of Arnold Palmer's most endearing qualities was his will to win. Despite his heartbreaking loss to Nicklaus in the 1962 playoff, Palmer fought back and was once again in contention for another Open crown. Nicklaus had missed the cut.

Amidst poor course conditions and an unpredictable swirling wind, Palmer, Julius Boros, the 1952 U.S. Open champion, and Jacky Cupit, a young pro from Texas, all tied at nine over par 293, the highest seventy-two hole score since 1935.

Both Palmer and Boros never expected to enter a playoff. As Cupit stood on the seventeenth tee of the final round he held a two-shot lead, needing only to play the final two holes in one over par to secure victory. But on the seventeenth he gave his entire lead away, making double-bogie six after slashing his way through the thick U.S. Open rough. To his credit on the eighteenth he still had a chance to win outright, but his twelve-foot birdie putt missed on the low side.

In the playoff on the following day Boros was in command from the beginning. One under par over the first five holes, he had opened up a three-shot lead. His front nine 33 maintained that advantage. And when Palmer made a triple-bogie seven on the eleventh, Boros was home free. His one under par 70 topped Cupit by three and Palmer by six.

Boros was forty-three years and three months old when he won the 1963 tournament, the oldest champion since the Englishman Ted Ray in 1920 and the oldest American ever to win the title.

1965: Bellerive Country Club, St. Louis, Missouri

Two milestones occurred at the 1965 U.S. Open: one changed the nature of the tournament, the other signaled the return of the foreign impact in the game.

Marginally influenced by the struggle of Ken Venturi in the intense heat of the 1964 Open and greatly regulated by the influx of television revenue, the USGA changed the tournament to a four-day event. Since 1926 the U.S. Open had been a three-day affair with the final thirty-six holes being played on Saturday. No other event in sport rivaled the drama of the final day in a U.S. Open. Now the tradition was gone and Venturi's courageous victory stood as the final testimony.

After 1920, when Ted Ray won the U.S. Open at the Inverness Club in Toledo, Ohio, no foreign player had won the championship. That forty-five-year streak came to an end in 1965 when Gary Player, a South African, and Kel Nagle, an Australian, tied for the championship and played off for the title. The signal from the foreign players had been sent.

In the tournament proper Player appeared to have victory well in hand with a three-shot lead and three holes remaining, owing chiefly to Nagle's double-bogie six on the par-four fifteenth. But a double-bogie five on the sixteenth by Player and a birdie by Nagle on the seventeenth resulted in a tie at the end of regulation with scores of 282.

The playoff provided no dramatics. Player was in charge from the start, mostly due to Nagle's wildness. He raced to a five-shot lead after eight holes and finished with a 71 to Nagle's 74.

Player's victory not only made him the first foreign champion in forty-five years but it also gave him a sweep of the four major championships, putting him in the lofty company of Gene Sarazen, Ben Hogan, and Jack Nicklaus. And, demonstrating his class and in remembrance of his youth, Player donated his entire winner's purse of $25,000 — $5,000 to cancer research and $20,000 to junior golf.

For Nagle it was a most disappointing loss. A popular player with both the fans and his fellow professionals, he enjoyed worldwide success as a professional golfer. His most shining moment came in 1960 when we won the 100th British Open at St. Andrews.

1966: Olympic Country Club, San Francisco, California

When the U.S. Open was first held at the Olympic Country Club in 1955, the tournament had bequeathed instant lore on the

Gary Player was victorious in a 1965 U.S. Open playoff at Bellerive over Kel Nagle.

San Francisco course with the upset playoff victory of Jack Fleck over Ben Hogan. The 1966 Open further added to that tradition.

For the third time in five years Arnold Palmer was involved in a playoff for the U.S. Open title — and lost. While Palmer had captivated fans with his aggressive, daring style, it was that same trait that led to his double collapse in the 1966 Open.

When the fourth round of the tournament began, Palmer held a three-stroke advantage over Billy Casper, the 1959 U.S. Open winner. And with a 32 on the front nine of the final day, he had structured a commanding seven-shot lead on Casper.

As he moved to the tenth tee, Palmer had confidently conceded the tournament to himself and set his sights on Ben Hogan's tournament record of 276 set in 1948. He needed only a one over par 35 on the inward nine for a 275.

He offset a bogie on ten with a birdie on twelve and still had a six-shot lead on Casper with six to play. But soon the lead had diminished to three with bogies on thirteen and fifteen against Casper's par and birdie. Palmer awoke to the Casper threat, yet always keeping the record in mind.

Needing a birdie now to beat Hogan, Palmer figured his best chance was on the par-five sixteenth. The birdie would also finish Casper. However, it was Casper who delivered the punch with a birdie four while Palmer slashed his way to an up and down bogie six from a greenside bunker. The lead now stood at one with two to play.

When Palmer bogied the par-four seventeenth and Casper parred, the two stood even with one to go. On the short but narrow eighteenth Palmer choose an iron from the tee. But his swing had left him and he hooked his shot into the left rough. Playing with the grit for which he was known, he carved a wedge through the thick rough to the back of the green some thirty feet above the hole, outside of Casper's ball.

When Palmer's first putt traveled six feet past the hole, it appeared the disaster would be complete. The pressure on Palmer was enormous for under a new rule he had to putt out before Casper would putt. If he missed, Casper could two-putt and win. But the Palmer legend held and he made the putt for par. Casper two-putted for his par and a tie at 278, two strokes above Hogan's record.

The playoff was a déjà vu of the previous afternoon. Palmer took command early shooting 33 to Casper's 35 on the front nine. Surely Palmer would hitch up his pants one more time and win the elusive second Open title?

But again he collapsed. A bogie at eleven against Casper's birdie evened the match and when Casper sank a fifty-footer for a birdie two on thirteen he was ahead for the first time. Mercifully, the end came quickly for Palmer when he played the next three in 5-5-7 to Casper's 4-3-6. At the end Casper had 69, Palmer 73. The collapse was final.

It was unfortunate that the focus of the tournament will always center on the tragedy of Palmer and not on the steady, determined play of Casper who captured his second U.S. Open title. The charismatic play of Palmer completely overshadowed the

Billy Casper was a two-time victor in playoffs. He won the 1966 U.S. Open at Olympic over Arnold Palmer and the 1970 Masters over Gene Littler.

consistent, calculated game of Casper, the type that is most often needed to win the Open.

1971: Merion Golf Club, Ardmore, Pennsylvania

There are occasions in golf when the perfect situation arises—great players competing on the most classic of golf courses for the title of a major championship. When the Open is held at

Merion, that postulate seems to always hold true. In 1971 two stars of the modern era, Lee Trevino and Jack Nicklaus, squared off in an eighteen hole playoff for the title after both had completed the regulation seventy-two holes at 280.

While Nicklaus had an opportunity to win the tournament on the last hole of regulation play when his fifteen-foot birdie putt skimmed the edge of the hole, it was the playoff that provided some great and some not so great golf.

Both played loosely at the start, Trevino bogieing the first and then Nicklaus hacking to a bogie and double bogie from bunkers on the second and third. Trevino was up by two.

Then suddenly each found his game. Nicklaus birdied the fifth, Trevino the eighth, then Nicklaus the ninth. At the turn it was Trevino 36, Nicklaus 37.

But the form that had returned so quickly for Nicklaus was lost again on the tenth, a short par four. After a perfect tee shot, he flubbed his approach short of the green and bogied. Trevino was up by two again.

Again Nicklaus regained his touch with a birdie on eleven. But Trevino wouldn't give in. He birdied twelve and then saved par on fourteen from eight feet.

The climax finally came on fifteen. With Trevino putting for birdie from twenty-five feet and Nicklaus from eight, it appeared that Jack might gain a stroke. But Trevino, appearing nerveless as always, rolled in his birdie. Nicklaus also made his, but his run was over. He could put no more pressure on Trevino. The final score: Trevino 68, Nicklaus 71.

But should anyone think the result was a fluke, Trevino went on to win the Canadian Open three weeks later and then in mid–July won the British Open. Three national championships within a month—a feat never equaled before or since.

1975: Medinah Country Club, Medinah, Illinois

The 1975 Open was the second hosted by Medinah. When the USGA visited in 1949, Cary Middlecoff captured the championship in regulation time. But 1975 was different.

Besides being marred with hot, humid weather and thunder-

Lee Trevino, the "Merry Mex," has appeared in only one playoff during his stellar career. He defeated Jack Nicklaus in a playoff for the 1971 U.S. Open title at Merion.

storms that turned the course into a quagmire, the twenty-sixth playoff in U.S. Open history featured two capable, yet unlikely, combatants — John Mahaffey, a young, rising star on the PGA Tour, and Lou Graham, a quiet, tour journeyman with two victories in eleven years.

Yet the real dramatic play came during the final eighteen holes of the tournament proper when one player after another with a chance to win the tournament fired and failed. Tom Watson, who had tied the Open's thirty-six hole record established by Mike Souchak in 1960, faded on Saturday with a 78 and then collapsed on Sunday with a 77. Frank Beard had grabbed the third round lead with a 67 on Saturday but on Sunday succumbed to the pressure with a 78.

Jack Nicklaus had won the Masters that year and talk of the professional Grand Slam was in the air again. Nicklaus stayed close to the lead all week so that when he birdied one, five, and nine on Sunday, he closed to within one shot of the lead. Alas, he too crumbled when he bogied the final three holes when three pars would have given him the Open by a shot. Ben Crenshaw, despite endangering squirrels with several tee shots during the week, came to the seventeenth, a 200-yard par three over water, tied with Graham and Beard. After a ten-minute wait on the tee Crenshaw's two iron was mishit and the ball came up short and in the water. He made double bogie after waiting another fifteen minutes to strike a twelve-foot bogie putt.

Graham came to the seventy-second hole needing only a par to win but bunkered his approach shot, played weakly from the bunker, and bogied to tie Mahaffey who had finished over one hour earlier at 287.

The playoff on the following day was demonstrative proof that golf is not a fair game nor equitable in its frustration. It also attested to the contention of some that golf can be a dull and boring game.

Mahaffey hit sixteen of eighteen greens in regulation and failed to make a birdie, shooting 73. Graham meanwhile birdied holes four, five, and ten and made a four on every hole of the back nine. The most spectacular came on the final hole. Leading by two shots he hooked his tee shot wildly and then played a low hook, five iron just short of the green. He got up and down for a four, an even par round of 71, and a two-shot victory.

Although he was sometimes criticized for his conservative

Lou Graham was victorious in a 1975 playoff for the U.S. Open at Medinah.

style of play, Graham had the last word in 1975. It was also a come-back of sorts for Graham. After a wrist injury and accompanying surgery in 1968, he battled his way back onto the tour in 1970. His conservative nature and quiet determination finally paid off in 1975.

1984: Winged Foot Golf Club, Mamaroneck, New York

That golf is a game to be played by sportsmen for sportsmen was never more evident than on the seventy-second hole of the 1984 Open. Most golf fans remember the final hole for what has been described by ABC's Jim McKay as "the sporting gesture of the year." It was most certainly that for, because of its uniqueness, it can never again be duplicated with the same impromptu, dramatic effect.

When third round leader Hale Irwin faded badly on the final day shooting 79, the contest was left to two of the most personable and likable players in the game, Fuzzy Zoeller, the easy-going, wise-cracking 1979 Masters champion and Greg Norman, a tall, strong, blonde Australian with a Palmer-like charisma.

With only the eighteenth remaining Zoeller and Norman were tied. But Norman was now playing shaky golf, having made scrambling pars on sixteen and seventeen after wild tee shots. Playing in the group directly in front of Zoeller, he knew a birdie was needed to force Zoeller's hand. And after a long, straight drive with only a six iron remaining, the possibility was real. But Norman's approach sailed some forty to fifty yards right of the green into the grandstands. After a free drop clear of the grandstands, his pitch flew to the far side of the green on the collar. Now, lying three about forty feet from the hole, a par was most unlikely.

As he surveyed his putt, Norman picked out a patch of brown grass about halfway to the hole as a directional mark. When the ball hit the patch, Norman knew the putt was in. The ball hit the flagstick dead center and fell in.

Meanwhile, Zoeller was back in the eighteenth fairway watching the dramatics transpire and thought the putt was for birdie. He had not witnessed Norman's cross-country adventure to the green, but he had observed Norman's two previous scrambling pars. He was forced to acknowledge the onslaught. He stepped to his bag, reached for his white towel, and waved it over his head in mock surrender. With one spontaneous gesture in an instant of time, Zoeller had forever etched his name in the history of golf.

But word quickly spread back from the green and Zoeller's gallery did attest that the putt was for par, not birdie. He accepted the challenge and parred the hole to force a tie at 276.

Fuzzy Zoeller has been unbeaten in playoffs. He defeated Tom Watson and Ed Sneed for the 1979 Masters title and then Greg Norman for the 1984 U.S. Open at Winged Foot.

The customary eighteen hole playoff was all but over on the second hole. Zoeller birdied from approximately seventy feet while Norman made double bogie. He never recovered. Zoeller continued to increase his lead and was out in 34 to Norman's 39. He finished with 67 to Norman's 75.

As the two came up the eighteenth fairway, Norman let Zoeller precede him, reached for his towel and reciprocated Zoeller's gesture of the previous day. They left the green with arms over shoulders.

1988: The Country Club, Brookline, Massachusetts

"Those who ignore history are doomed to repeat it."

When the USGA scheduled the 1988 U.S. Open for The Country Club in Brookline, Massachusetts, they certainly should have expected a playoff, most likely a three-way encounter. In the two previous Opens played at The Country Club, 1913 and 1963, three-way ties had resulted. In 1988 the USGA was fortunate, in the end only two remained for the playoff.

At a time when world dominance of the game had seemingly shifted from the United States to the foreign scene, Curtis Strange, with definite claims to being the premiere U.S. player, faced Nick Faldo, the reigning British Open champion in an eighteen hole playoff after the pair had tied at the end of seventy-two holes with 278 (− 6).

The playoff presented Strange with two decidedly personal opportunities: first, with a victory he could rightly claim to be one of the top players on the world golf scene. For several years golf experts had predicted greatness for Strange who possessed one of the most stellar amateur records in years. When he turned professional in 1976, he had won virtually every major amateur championship in the United States except the U.S. Amateur where twice he had been beaten in late rounds by the eventual champion.

On the PGA Tour he had experienced financial and personal success, highlighted by twelve victories in ten years through 1987. Nevertheless, there were no major championships on his record.

All of which leads to his second opportunity and probably most important to Curtis Strange the person. In the 1985 Masters

Strange had rebounded from an opening round 80 with second and third day scores of 65 and 68. So complete was his comeback that he had built a three-shot lead with only six holes to play in the tournament. But disaster struck on the thirteenth and fifteenth when he hit into the water on both and eventually lost the tournament to Bernhard Langer of West Germany.

It can safely be said that in the 1988 U.S. Open Strange was on a mission to fulfill a dream. Once content with the singular goal of making money, he no longer wanted to be known as a money-making machine. Now he also wanted to be labeled as a great player.

What stood between Strange and his dream was the 1987 British Open champion, Nick Faldo. Faldo had captured that tournament by wearing down the opposition on the final day with eighteen straight pars to edge American Paul Azinger by one stroke.

But before these two could play out the high drama of the playoff, the final round had to be contested.

Beginning the final eighteen, Strange held a tenuous one-stroke lead over Faldo, Bob Gilder, and the 1987 U.S. Open champion Scott Simpson. One shot farther back was 1987 Masters champion Larry Mize. But one by one all but Strange and Faldo vanished. Finally Strange came to the seventy-second hole needing a par to tie Faldo. When he bunkered his second in front of the green, the pressure intensified. With the skill of a surgeon, he blasted to three feet and holed the putt.

The playoff was a test of raw nerve with both players starting out sloppily. Gradually the players settled in and Strange birdied the fifth and seventh to take a one-stroke lead after nine. Strange gained another stroke at the tenth when Faldo took three from the edge but gave it back to the twelfth.

It was Strange who eventually got the big break at the thirteenth, when Faldo three-putted for bogie and he "wished" in a twelve-footer for birdie. His lead was now three with five to go. Faldo fought back immediately with a birdie at the par-five fourteenth to cut the margin to two. At the fifteenth both made nervous looking bogies and followed with pars at sixteen.

At last the historic seventeenth. Faldo's approach flew over the green and Strange found the right, greenside bunker. Strange had the better play and played his sand shot to four feet. Faldo's chip was like downhill linoleum and the closest he could stop it was ten feet. Faldo missed and Strange sank. The eighteenth was anticlimactic —

Curtis Strange captured the first of two consecutive U.S. Open titles in a playoff over Nick Faldo in 1988 at The Country Club.

Strange making par for 71 and Faldo making a bogie for 75. Curtis Strange had finally elevated himself to superstar.

1990: Medinah Country Club, Medinah, Illinois

In 1990 the USGA and its premier event, the U.S. Open attained a milestone in playoff history. Never before had the championship winner been determined by sudden-death. The ultimate result of that policy was the marathon, 144 hole battle in 1931 between Billy Burke and George Von Elm. But since then the USGA had modified its policy to the point where any ties after the championship proper would be determined by an eighteen hole playoff the following day. Any ties resulting from the eighteen hole playoff would be settled in a sudden-death format. The USGA's worst fears became a reality in 1990.

After ninety holes of golf over Medinah's modified number three course, Hale Irwin, a two-time U.S. Open champion, and Mike Donald, a career nonwinner, still remained tied. Through seventy-two holes of regulation play they had each shot 280 (− 8). Over the eighteen holes of the playoff they had deadlocked at 74 (+ 2). The decision was finally settled in sudden-death when Irwin holed a ten-foot birdie putt on the first hole.

Since Medinah last hosted the U.S. Open in 1975, the course had undergone a moderate facelift. At the suggestion of the USGA, who strongly hinted that the Open would not be played at Medinah again until certain changes were made, the club constructed new holes for the seventeenth and eighteenth and redesigned the fourteenth hole to become a par five. The result was the awarding of the 1990 U.S. Open by the USGA.

Not only was the revised Medinah course under a microscope, but Curtis Strange was also. Trying for a third consecutive U.S. Open title, Strange was closely watched the entire week. Despite the enormous pressure, he maneuvered himself into contention after Saturday's third round trailing the leaders by only two shots. But on Sunday he found his tank empty and he faltered to a 75, finishing six shots behind Irwin and Donald.

Sunday, however, was not without its dramatics, most of them provided by the forty-five-year-old Irwin. Of twenty-nine players that began the final round within five shots of the coleaders Donald and Billy Ray Brown, only Irwin and Masters champion Nick Faldo were able to endure the last day pressures and threaten the leaders.

Irwin began the final round four shots behind and gained no ground after an even par 36 on the front line. Then he zeroed in. With precision iron play he birdied eleven through fourteen with putts that totaled no more than twenty-five feet. Unable to birdie sixteen or seventeen with putts of twelve and eight feet, he came to the eighteenth seven under par for the tournament and still trailing Donald, who was playing almost nine holes behind him, by two. Reaching the green in two, he was faced with a sixty-foot, roller-coaster birdie putt. The putt seemed to roll forever. Finally it disappeared. And so did Irwin. Normally placid in his emotions on the

One of the truly great U.S. Open champions. In 1990 Hale Irwin won his third U.S. Open title when he defeated Mike Donald in a playoff that extended to sudden-death on the 19th playoff hole.

course, he took off in a victory lap around the green giving high fives to a platoon of gallery members.

Faldo was bidding to keep his Grand Slam hopes alive. And for a while it looked like he might succeed. With birdies on eleven and fourteen he stood at eight under. But a three putt on sixteen dropped him one back. On the seventy-second hole he faced a twenty-footer to tie Irwin. The putt looked in all the way but at the last instant grazed the right edge of the cup and stayed out. Once again there would be no Grand Slam.

Brown played consistently most of the day and when he birdied the difficult par-three seventeenth from two feet, he went to seven under and a chance to tie Irwin and Donald. On eighteen he left himself a fifteen-foot birdie try, but badly misread the putt, finished with a par, and a third place tie with Faldo.

Donald tenaciously held to his one-shot lead throughout the

back nine thanks to par-saving putts on twelve and fourteen from twenty-five feet and fifteen feet respectively. He finally cracked at the sixteenth when his second shot found a bunker and he failed to sink a twelve-foot par putt. With pars on seventeen and eighteen he finished tied with Irwin, setting up Monday's showdown.

Irwin took command early in the playoff and led by one shot after eight holes. But the momentum switched at the ninth when Irwin bogied and Donald birdied. Donald gained another stroke at the twelfth when Irwin bogied. The lead was now two shots with six holes to play. Both players birdied the par-five fourteenth and then parred the fifteenth. Irwin was still two down with just three to play.

But he saved his best shot of the day for the sixteenth. Playing into the wind, Irwin hooked a two iron around overhanging trees to six feet and made the birdie. Both players parred seventeen and Donald still led by one on the eighteenth tee. But he faltered off the tee and hooked his drive into the trees. He played his second into the bunker in front of the green and his third finished fifteen feet away. After Irwin had made a routine par, Donald stood over his putt. The stroke was good, but the ball failed to drop.

The first sudden-death in U.S. Open history began at the first hole, a 385-yard par four. Both players hit good drives from the tee. Donald played first from the fairway, the ball stopping thirty feet short on the green. Irwin came next and lofted a sand wedge to ten feet. Donald's first putt stopped one foot short. Irwin's putt did not. The ball rolled into the dead center of the hole.

Irwin's victory made him only the fifth player to win more than two Opens. He joined the company of Willie Anderson, Bobby Jones, Ben Hogan, and Jack Nicklaus. At an age of forty-five years and fifteen days, he became the oldest Open winner, passing Ray Floyd who won in 1986 at forty-three years, nine months, eleven days. But most amazingly he became the first player to win the Open after receiving a special exemption to participate from the USGA. His ten-year exemption following his 1979 victory had lapsed in 1990, but the USGA invited him to play. It was the best decision they had made since permitting sudden-death.

4
PGA

The Professional Golfers Association was brought into existence through the efforts of Rodman Wanamaker. The Philadelphia department store magnate wanted to bring a sense of dignity to the professional and simultaneously stimulate a growth in the game which had received a major boost with Francis Ouimet's victory in the U.S. Open just three years earlier in 1913. Wanamaker fully realized that an organization of professional golfers would serve to elevate the profession from second-class status.

To create initial interest he proposed an annual match play tournament modeled after the British News of the World tournament. He also supplied the prize money, the trophies, and medals.

From its rudimentary beginning, October 10–14, 1916, at the Siwanoy Country Club in Bronxville, the PGA Championship has enjoyed distinction in both its format and its champions. The tournament continued as a match play event through 1957 with the finale always scheduled for thirty-six holes. In 1958 the PGA adopted the more spectator suitable, television adaptable, and financially profitable stroke play format for its competition. And, despite an occasional outcry from the purists of the game for a return to its original match play format, it has remained so ever since.

While the change to stroke play was no doubt financially beneficial to the PGA, it was also a relief to the professionals. Under the match play format the two finalists would play up to nine rounds of golf in five days. This demanding and exhausting physical ordeal sometimes caused the better known players to skip the tournament, despite the fact that it was a major championship.

With entry into the tournament reserved strictly for professional golfers, many professionals, both touring and club pros, believe it is *the* major championship to win, for the victor is deemed to be at the top of his profession. The winner is indeed the best professional golfer. It is for this reason that the winners of the PGA Championship stand out as a who's who of professional golf.

In accordance with its original match play format, there was, of course, no possibility of a tie in regulation play and thus a playoff for the championship. But, if you prefer, each final thirty-six hole match was indeed a two-man playoff in its own right.

With the adoption of stroke play in 1958, the possibility of a playoff became a distinct reality. However, it was not until 1961, the fourth year of stroke play, that the tournament experienced its first extra holes. Of the six playoffs that have occurred to date in the PGA, only the first two were conducted over eighteen holes. When the need for the third playoff arose in 1977, the format had been changed to a hole-by-hole sudden-death.

Finally, at the end of the 1989 championship, the PGA announced that it was considering settlement of all future ties at the end of the regulation seventy-two holes with a four hole playoff, with the lowest aggregate score determining the winner — the same format currently in use at the British Open and first tested in 1989 with great success.

1961: Olympia Fields Country Club, Chicago, Illinois

Olympia Fields Country Club, lying in the suburbs of Chicago, was a unique test for the PGA Championship. Measuring 6,722 yards and playing to a par of 70, the tournament conducted over its eighteen holes came to an breathtaking and dramatic finish.

If the theory that great putting can overcome great shot making holds any merit, the 1961 PGA serves as a prime example.

With three holes remaining in the final round of regulation play, the diminutive Jerry Barber trailed Don January by four shots. Barber then began a string of miraculous, multiple putts by sinking putts of twenty feet for birdie, forty feet for par, and sixty feet for birdie to equal January's seventy-two hole total of 277.

In the eighteen hole playoff held the following day, Barber again produced the miraculous. Despite trailing by two shots on two different occasions, he rallied to win by one shot, 67–68, when once again he sank a sixty-foot putt on the last green to win his only major championship.

Standing only five feet five inches tall and weighing a slight 135 pounds, Barber at age forty-five became the smallest and at the time the oldest to win the PGA Championship. It was solace for the man who just two years previously appeared to have the PGA title won until he bogied the final two holes.

1967: Columbine Country Club, Denver, Colorado

Six years passed before a second playoff was required in the stroke play version of the PGA Championship. But it was not only the championship itself that made the visit to the Columbine Country Club in suburban Denver memorable. Controversy threatened the very playing of the tournament itself.

The championship came at a time when the relationship between the touring professionals and the PGA of America was more ceremonious than official. At issue was the percentage of television revenues to be counted in the tournament prize monies. At a time of greatly increased television receipts, this was serious money. The touring professionals even threatened to boycott the event. Fortunately, a compromise was reached and the tournament was played as scheduled.

But the relationship would never be the same. The following year the Tournament Players Division of the PGA was formed and the rift would forever remain visibly evident.

To add to the woes of the PGA Jack Nicklaus grumbled about the scheduling of the PGA Championship which followed the heels of the British Open. He also mentioned that the quality of the courses selected by the PGA for its championship was somewhat less than championship caliber.

The PGA listened. In 1969 the championship was moved to dates in August, and in 1970 the PGA began to use a rotation of top quality courses for play in the tournament.

Through all of this the Columbine Country Club simply wanted to play host to the PGA Championship. It appeared it might never get to do so. The tournament was originally scheduled for the suburban Denver layout in 1966 but a 1965 flood destroyed hundreds of trees and several greens. Unable to restore the course for the 1966 tournament, the PGA awarded the 1967 championship to Columbine. Then, controversy aside, one week before the 1967 event the course was heavily damaged by a hailstorm that left the greens pitted and virtually unplayable. Fortunately, the weather remained inclement and the ensuing rain softened the greens making them playable for the tournament.

For the uninitiated golf in the thin mountain air can be a bewildering and sometimes frustrating experience as many in the field discovered. Oddly, two Texas flatlanders, Don January and Don Massengale, tied at the end of seventy-two holes with 281.

In the PGA's second and final eighteen hole playoff, January, who had previously lost in a playoff for the 1961 PGA Championship, captured his first and only major championship. He led by two shots at the turn and maintained that margin throughout the back nine, winning 69 to 71.

For January the victory was the culmination of a consistent and successful career that included eleven PGA Tour wins. He won the Dallas Open in his rookie year and, after a short respite from 1972 to 1975 when he tried his hand at course design, he returned to the tour and captured the 1976 Tournament of Champions. He also holds the distinction of being the oldest player to compete in the Ryder Cup matches, a biannual competition between the best European professionals and the best professionals of the United States.

1977: Pebble Beach Golf Links, Monterey, California

It was another ten years before the third playoff and the first with a sudden-death format took place in the PGA. For the first time in the stroke play history of the event, the setting moved to the west coast to the fabled Pebble Beach Golf Links on the Monterey Peninsula.

Playing to just over 6,800 yards, Pebble Beach is unique among American golf courses, not only because it is old-fashioned in design but also because of its setting. Situated on the rocky cliffs of Carmel Bay some 120 miles south of San Francisco, the course features small, well-contoured greens with a minimum of strategic

Don January won the 1967 PGA Championship in a playoff over Don Massengale at Columbine, outside Denver.

bunkering. Built in the early 1920s under architect Jack Neville, the course attained national notoriety when it became the site for the annual Bing Crosby National Pro-Amateur Championship (now the AT&T Pro-Am).

When the unpredictable weather takes a turn for the worse and the winds arise along Carmel Bay, the fourth through the eighth—a stretch of holes along the coast—can play as difficult as any in the world. Holes such as the short 120-yard seventh can require a long iron or even a wood to reach the green which measures only eight yards in width. And the ninth, a long 450-yard par four, is virtually unreachable in two by most players.

In the 1977 PGA the seventy-two holes of regulation play ended in a two-way deadlock at 282 (−6) between Lanny Wadkins and

Gene Littler. Littler, who had won the 1975 Bing Crosby Pro-Am over this same course, uncharacteristically lost a five-shot lead over the last nine holes of regulation play when he bogied five of the first six holes on the back side. Littler's freefall allowed Jack Nicklaus to draw even with Wadkins just one shot behind. But when Nicklaus bogied the seventeenth and Wadkins birdied the eighteenth, it was Wadkins and Littler who headed for sudden-death.

The playoff, which was won by Wadkins with a birdie on the third hole, marked the first time that a major championship had been decided by sudden-death encounter. Just as the switch to stroke play in 1958 had been predicated by television, likewise the change to sudden-death was also the byproduct of television and the demands of an impatient society for an instant winner.

1978: Oakmont Country Club, Oakmont, Pennsylvania

There are certain major championships which hold an eternal jinx over great players. Sam Snead in the U.S. Open and Arnold Palmer in the PGA are two of the more recognizable examples. Tom Watson is also a victim of the PGA.

This was vividly portrayed at the sixty-first PGA Championship held at the Oakmont Country Club, the previous host to five U.S. Open championships and two match play PGA championships.

For three rounds Watson had played essentially flawless golf on one of the most difficult of the U.S. golf courses. With three rounds of 67, 69, and 67, Watson held a commanding five-shot lead over Jerry Pate entering the final round. John Mahaffey was another two behind.

Oakmont, which many consider the toughest course in the world, excluding those affected by weather, was the dream become reality of steel magnate Henry C. Fownes. It has several distinguishing features.

First, it is renowned for its large and fast greens. After initial construction, they were rolled with quarter-ton barrels of sand and are continually cut to a height of one-sixteenth of an inch. And because of their enormous size, a player may reach a green in regulation, but had no guarantee that par is a surety.

Second, nearly 200 bunkers of the original 220 still remain and

traverse the landscape, perhaps the most famous being the Church Pew bunker between the third and fourth fairways. And, as an additional torment to the player, each bunker is raked with a specially designed instrument (resembling a rake) to create furrows two inches deep and two inches apart.

The third distinguishing feature is the Pennsylvania Turnpike which separates holes two through eight from the rest of the course. Fortunately for Fownes, the construction of the turnpike, which came after the course had been constructed, had no effect on the course. Previous construction of a railroad many years earlier had created a gorge and the turnpike simply followed the railroad through the gorge.

Although Watson had struggled briefly on the front nine of the final day, he still maintained a four-stroke margin with nine to play. But when he doubled-bogied the tenth, he slowly began to unravel. By the time he reached the seventeenth tee, he had slipped one behind Pate and Mahaffey who were tied for the lead.

But Watson is forever the fighter. Anchoring himself one more time, he birdied the seventeenth, only to be counterpunched by Pate with his own birdie to keep the margin at one. And when Pate was safely on the final green in two and Watson and Mahaffey could not produce the needed birdies for an apparent tie, the outcome seemed little in doubt.

But, unexplainably, after a somewhat inadequate approach putt, Pate missed his short par putt, watching the ball spin back at him after skimming the edge of the hole and sending the championship to a three-way sudden-death, the first in PGA history.

Although he had put together a magnificent 66 in the final round, Mahaffey was still regarded as the underdog. In the time since his disheartening 1975 U.S. Open playoff loss to Lou Graham at Medinah, Mahaffey had been plagued by wrist and back injuries which threatened to end his career forever. He had fallen from the position of being one of the PGA tour's most consistent performers to the ranks of the journeyman.

Pate, on the other hand, was regarded as the new wonder boy of golf, having followed a stellar amateur career that included the 1974 U.S. Amateur Championship with a dramatic victory in the 1976 U.S. Open. Watson, of course, was already in the arena of the

Opposite: Lanny Wadkins appeared in two playoffs, both in the PGA. In 1977 he defeated Gene Littler, but fell to Larry Nelson in 1987.

Although he amassed eight major championships, Tom Watson was never victorious in a major championship playoff. He fell to Fuzzy Zoeller in the 1979 Masters and John Mahaffey in the 1978 PGA Championship, the one major he has not won.

John Mahaffey had one win and one loss in major championship play-offs. In 1978 he defeated Tom Watson and Jerry Pate to win the PGA Championship at Oakmont, Pennsylvania.

superstar with two British Open titles and one Masters coming into the 1978 season. And despite Pate's faux pas at the last and Watson's sudden collapse over the last nine, there was little dissent that the title would be decided between the two.

On the first hole of the sudden-death playoff, all three made nervous, scrambling pars. The second hole at Oakmont is a short par four that demands all of a player's accuracy from the tee. Watson and Pate drove with irons, but Mahaffey, the shortest hitter of the three, was forced to play a three wood. Away for the second shot, Mahaffey lofted a nine iron to twelve feet above the cup, leaving a downhill-sidehill putt for birdie. Watson played a wedge to thirty-five feet, but Pate missed the green and his pitch still left him seven feet for par.

Watson could do no better than par. Mahaffey sensed the kill. He delicately stroked his downhiller into the dead center of the hole for the championship.

Once again the giant had been slayed.

1979: Oakland Hills Country Club, Birmingham, Michigan

The 1979 PGA Championship provided unexpected seventy-second hole dramatics as well as sudden-death playoff suspense.

Coming to the final hole of regulation play, Australian David Graham needed only a par four for a final round, seven under par 63 over Oakland Hills's par 70, 7,014 yard layout and a two-shot victory. But Graham, who had played impeccable golf through the first seventeen holes in eliminating a four-shot lead held by journeyman pro Rex Caldwell, inexplicably could not find the fairway and struggled to a double-bogie six and a seventy-two hole tie with Ben Crenshaw at 272 (− 8).

Crenshaw, the prodigy from Texas, was still looking for his first major title since joining the tour in 1973 and seemed the favorite over the distraught Graham. And indeed it appeared that Crenshaw had the victory in hand on the first extra hole until Graham rolled in an eighteen-foot par putt to tie. Graham's putting magic struck again on the second when he tied Crenshaw with a ten-foot birdie. Graham mercifully completed the kill with another one-putt for a birdie two on the third extra hole. Victory had been snatched from the jaws of defeat.

1987: PGA National Golf Club, Palm Beach Gardens, Florida

The 1987 PGA Championship returned to its "home course" at the challenging Champion course inside the PGA National Golf Club in Palm Beach Gardens, Florida. The weather for this tournament was as much the story as the quality of golf over a long and difficult layout, made even more hazardous by thick Bermuda rough that in most cases allowed a player only a wedge shot back to safety. The conditions were made even more arduous by greens

David Graham won a sudden-death victory over Ben Crenshaw for the 1979 PGA Championship at Oakland Hills.

that were pitted due to some ill-fated maintenance procedures one month before the tournament.

With temperatures hovering in the 90s and humidity to match, only Larry Nelson and Lanny Wadkins, both seasoned veterans and both former PGA champions, survived the heat and the golf course to enter the sudden-death playoff.

The tournament proper turned into an interesting free-for-all on the last day of regulation with play at times taking on the look of a comedy of errors.

Nelson started the day three strokes behind the leaders and after a bogie on the second he birdied the third and fourth and followed with nine consecutive pars.

Mark McCumber slashed his way through the Bermuda rough to a front nine of 40 while others such as Lanny Wadkins (37), Ben Crenshaw (38), Bobby Wadkins (40), Seve Ballesteros (40), and Ray Floyd (42) found the greens and rough little more to their liking.

Larry Nelson was victorious in his one playoff appearance in 1987 in the PGA Championship. Nelson defeated Lanny Wadkins at PGA National.

Eventually they all bunched together on the back nine and at one juncture five players were tied at minus one. Scott Hoch had moved into the picture with a front nine of 34 and birdies on eleven, twelve, and thirteen. Playing one hour in front of the leaders, Hoch came to the seventy-second hole and faced an eight-foot putt for birdie which would put him in the clubhouse at 287 (−2). He quickly proceeded to three putt when even a simple two putt would have put him in the eventual playoff.

Nelson came to the final hole after having just holed a twenty-foot birdie putt on the seventy-first hole. Three precise shots to the par-five last hole left him with a thirty-footer for birdie. The ball stopped one inch short and he finished with a 72 for the day and a 287 (−1) total.

Lanny Wadkins came to the final hole with a round that included two double bogies, two bogies, and five birdies. At the last hole he two-putted from twenty feet to join Nelson at minus one.

The last threat was Mark McCumber. Needing a birdie on the final hole to make the playoff a three-way affair, McCumber reached for his driver on his second shot. A brief moment of indecision caused him to replace the club but he quickly grabbed it again. The shot sailed a bit right and caught the water. Yet, he still had one more swing to make a four. His wedge shot from 120 yards spun back over the edge of the hole. The playoff would be for two, beginning at the tenth.

After safe drives on the par-four tenth, both missed the green on their second shots. Wadkins was to the right and Nelson over the back edge. Facing an uphill chip, Wadkins skidded the ball five feet past the hole. Nelson played his shot to about six and one-half feet. Nelson's putt for par was dead center and the pressure was on Wadkins. His putt was solid but skidded over the right edge of the hole, giving Nelson his second PGA Championship.

Larry Nelson is somewhat of an anomaly in the game of golf. He did not begin the game until the age of twenty-two, the point in life when most young college players are just turning professional. After a time in the military and a tour in Vietnam, Nelson took up the game of golf in 1969. Within two years he was a professional and in 1973 he became a member of the PGA Tour. Twelve years after learning the game he won his first major championship, the 1981 PGA. In 1983 he won the U.S. Open at Oakmont. With his playoff victory he became the fourth player to win three majors in the 1980s along with Ballesteros, Watson, and Nicklaus.

5
Masters

The Masters is the Masters. What more can one say? Played during the first full week of April each year, it has come to symbolize the beginning of golf season. It is golf's rite of passage into spring.

While it is the youngest of the four major championships, it was, nevertheless, destined for importance by the very presence of its founder—the immortal Bobby Jones.

The tournament began in 1934, four years after Jones had effectively retired from competitive golf. He was the man and the impetus behind the event.

The Masters is unique in that it is the one major championship annually conducted over the same golf course, the internationally famous Augusta National Golf Club in Georgia.

Despite the spectacular record of competitive golf that Bobby Jones left behind, the August National Golf Club will always remain as his legacy. Set amidst the dogwoods and pines of Georgia with a generous sprinkling of azaleas, the course stands as a monument to a true legend of the game.

Designed by Jones, a player who knew shot values like no other, and the Scottish architect Alister Mackenzie, a golf course designer who had the knack of maintaining natural beauty while creating spectacular and challenging golf, the Augusta National features gentle, rolling hills, wide fairways, and large, undulating greens.

While the course that Jones and Mackenzie initially created has undergone many changes, it remains essentially the same today. It is still the ultimate "thinking man's" golf course. With the slightest mental lapse the player will be smitten with a bogie or worse. Each shot must be played with forethought and great precision, even on the seemingly wide fairways.

The most famous grouping of holes at Augusta National is Amen Corner, a stretch of three holes encompassing the par-four eleventh, the par-three twelfth, and the par-five thirteenth that are threatened by Rae's Creek, a meandering brook that promises trouble at its every turn. Each shot must be struck with the touch of a surgeon. It is here that the Masters is often won or lost on Sunday afternoon. The list of tragedies at Amen Corner is morose indeed.

The Masters was not originally conceived with the intent of becoming a major championship. No tournament can realistically expect that status to be thrust upon it. Initially, it was simply a gathering of a few of Jones's golfing friends to test their skills against his new course and enjoy the camarderie of the game itself. It was known simply as the "Augusta National Invitation Tournament." But fate would not be denied. In the second year of the event, the "shot heard 'round the world" was struck and the tournament was catapulated into major status almost immediately. In 1938 it became known as "The Masters."

The tournament has always been conducted as a seventy-two hole stroke play event. Of the fifty-four championships conducted through 1990, only eleven have resulted in a playoff. Because of the composition of the field, which is strictly determined by invitation only, each playoff has included at least one established star of the game. This fact alone provides the tournament with tradition and legend.

Initially all playoffs for the championship were scheduled to be held at thirty-six holes. However, only one playoff was ever held at that distance. When the second playoff arose in 1942, the length had been shortened to eighteen holes, a distance at which five playoffs were conducted. Then in 1976 the Masters became the first major championship to officially switch to a sudden-death format. All playoffs now begin at the par-four tenth, the entrance to Amen Corner.

1935

The 1935 Masters, which was won by Gene Sarazen over Craig Wood in a thirty-six hole playoff, is forged into golf history not because of the playoff, but rather for one incredible shot that brought about the tie.

The legendary Gene Sarazen who was involved in two playoffs. The most famous was the 1935 Masters where he gained a tie for the title with a double eagle on the 15th. He easily defeated Craig Wood for the championship.

"The shot" was a four wood second that found the cup on the par-five fifteenth for a double eagle. Sarazen had come to the fifteenth tee needing three birdies in the final four holes to tie Wood. With one shot he had made the three birdies.

The press immediately dubbed the accomplishment "the shot hear 'round the world." Indeed, it was—for two distinct reasons.

First, but certainly second in importance, the shot enabled

Sarazen to immediately erase his three-shot deficit and force a playoff. Wood had already finished and was being hailed by all as the winner.

Second, and most important, that shot, together with the fact that the Masters was Bobby Jones's tournament played over his personally designed course, propelled the event to instant notoriety.

The significant factor was the timing. As Charles Price has so ably noted in his book, *A Golf Story*, the nation was in the midst of a depression and willing to firmly grasp any good news, regardless of the scenario. Sarazen's shot provided an emotional lift to the entire country.

The shot occurred in the second year of the Masters. The double eagle was essentially the final thrust to putting the Masters in the line with the other majors, despite its young age. Not only did it have a worthy founder, an elite field, and a top quality championship course, but now it also had instant history, lore, and tradition.

Of course, the fact that the miracle was produced by Gene Sarazen, one of the greatest players the game has seen, was not detrimental to the cause. Any tournament that is rich with the names of such great players as Hogan, Nelson, Snead, Player, Nicklaus, and Watson inscribed on its championship trophy is automatically elevated one notch higher than the average everyday PGA Tour event. Prior to 1934 Sarazen had amassed the two U.S. Opens (1922, 1932), one British Open (1932), and three PGA Championships (1922, 1923, 1933). With his victory he became the first professional to capture the professional Grand Slam — the U.S. Open, the British Open, the PGA, and the Masters. He was, at the time of the 1934 Masters, already a legend of the game.

For the record, the playoff was held on thirty-six holes the following day. Sarazen won by five shots, 144 to 149.

1942

There are certain fortunate times in the game of golf that a classic head-to-head confrontation for a major championship occurs. It is, in a sense, the ideal match race. Such was the case in the playoff for the 1942 Masters title, Byron Nelson opposing Ben Hogan. Two of the greatest players the game has produced in a one-on-one competition for a major championship.

Byron Nelson captured two Masters titles in playoffs, 1939 and 1942. He lost a U.S. Open playoff in 1946 to Lloyd Mangrum.

What made this confrontation even more intriguing was the fact that Hogan and Nelson were boyhood friends from Fort Worth, Texas. They had learned the game together in the caddy yards of Fort Worth and come up to the professional ranks at the same time. And, although Hogan's game matured later than Nelson's, the rivalry was forever evident.

The playoff was a supreme example of top quality golf under extreme pressure. Yet it began inauspiciously for Nelson who pushed his tee shot on the opening hole way right and suffered a double bogie, dropping two shots to Hogan immediately. Through the first five holes Hogan led by three and continued his excellent play over the next eleven, shooting one under par. But amazingly, during that eleven hole stretch, he lost five strokes to Nelson who played them six under. Nelson's incredible streak included a birdie at six, an eagle on the par-five eighth, and then a spectacular run of three consecutive birdies at Amen Corner—eleven, twelve, and thirteen.

But Hogan did not crumble. He fought back with birdies on fourteen and fifteen, only to be cut off by Nelson who birdied the par-three sixteenth from four feet. In the end Nelson escaped with a one-shot victory, 69 to 70.

The combination of top quality golf produced under the pressure of a major championship by two of the game's finest players only served to pique the interest of the golfing public even more. The founder of the tournament could never be forgotten and the caliber of the champions which the event produced elevated the tournament to the top rung of the prestige ladder.

1954

In 1954 the mystique of the Masters prevailed once more. While the playoff for the title was between the two most prolific players of the game at that time, Ben Hogan, the defending champion, and Sam Snead, the real story of the 1954 Masters was an amateur, Billy Joe Patton from Morganton, North Carolina.

In any other year a playoff confrontation between Hogan and Snead would have been the leading golf story of the year. But by the time the playoff ensued, much of the emotion of the tournament had been drained by the performance of Patton.

After leading through the first two rounds, Patton had slipped

back on the third day and fallen five shots behind Hogan. Snead
had moved between them, just three behind Hogan. But Patton
was destined for his fifteen minutes of fame. In a remarkable
stretch of holes on the final day, Patton aced the par-three sixth,
parred the seventh, and then birdied the eighth and ninth to draw
even with Hogan.

Even then, the playoff might not have come about were it not
for Hogan's challenge to the par-four eleventh on his second shot.
Patton had just taken a double-bogie seven on the thirteenth after
hitting his ball into Rae's Creek which cuts in front of the green.
But Hogan, who was famous for isolating himself from all distrac-
tions on a golf course, did not pick up from his own gallery that Patton had made the double bogie. On the eleventh he aimed for the
pin set on the left-hand side of the green and hit the ball in the
water. He stumbled to a double-bogie six and finished the round
with 75 to tie Snead. Patton, still playing all-or-nothing golf, hit his
second shot on the fifteenth into the water and bogied. He eventually finished a stroke behind Snead and Hogan.

When the playoff ensued on the following day, Hogan and
Snead played dead even at 35 through the first nine holes. Snead
edged ahead on the tenth with a chip-in for birdie, but Hogan
gained it back on the eleventh. Snead pulled ahead again by a
stroke with a birdie on the thirteenth.

The decision was settled on the par-three sixteenth. After
both hit the green Snead two-putted and awaited Hogan. Hogan's
first putt was miserable, five feet short. He missed the next. And
even though he gained a stroke on the eighteenth, he lost the playoff by a one stroke.

Hogan had played a masterful round of precision golf, hitting
all eighteen greens in regulation while Snead was hitting just thirteen. Yet Hogan lost the playoff 70 to 71. In the end it was his always suspect putting that had been his undoing.

This was the only meeting between Hogan and Snead in a
playoff for a major championship, although Snead did defeat
Hogan two other times in playoffs.

1962

In the 1962 Masters Arnold Palmer had a score to settle. Coming to the seventy-second hole of the 1961 tournament, he needed

Sam Snead was involved in only two playoffs. His one victory came in a classic battle with Ben Hogan in the 1954 Masters.

Although passed his prime in this picture, Arnold Palmer was a frequent participant in playoffs. However, his record of one win and three losses was unspectacular. His lone playoff victory came in the 1962 Masters.

only a par to be the first repeat champion of the event. His approach had found the right, greenside bunker from where he made double-bogie six, losing to Gary Player by one shot.

Palmer's victory in 1962 was typically Palmeresque. Beginning the final day with a two-shot lead over Dow Finsterwald and a four-stroke margin over Gary Player, Palmer played the first fifteen holes in five over par. When he reached the sixteenth tee, he was two behind Finsterwald and Player. But in true Palmer style he birdied two of the last three holes, including a delicate forty-five foot, downhill chip-in on the par-three sixteenth to tie defending champion Gary Player and Dow Finsterwald at 280.

In the playoff Palmer again came from behind. Trailing Player by three shots after nine holes (Finsterwald was never a factor), Palmer again produced the charge which earmarked his career. Beginning the back nine, he birdied ten, twelve, thirteen, and fourteen. This masterful streak carried him from a three-shot deficit to a four-shot lead. He finished with a five under par 31 on the back nine for a 68 to Player's 71 and Finsterwald's 77.

Palmer's victory made him the third three-time winner of the Masters title, following in the footsteps of Jimmy Demaret and Sam Snead. Curiously, his victories had all come in even-numbered years, 1958, 1960, and 1962.

1966

The first player to repeat as the Masters's champion was, not unexpectedly, Jack Nicklaus. In his only appearance in a Masters playoff, Nicklaus captured a three-way decision over Tommy Jacobs and Gay Brewer.

The 1966 tournament was plagued by high scores throughout, resulting from two quirks of nature. A late spring cold spell had left the usually immaculate Augusta National course in less than superb condition. This was further complicated by unusually high winds that made playing conditions most difficult and unpredictable.

The unmanageable conditions made for a wide open tournament with no less than seventeen players either holding the lead or tying for it at various times. But in the end only three remained.

In the playoff, which laboriously took over five hours to complete, Nicklaus finally pulled away at the eleventh with a long birdie putt. His final score of 70 bested Jacobs by two and Brewer by eight.

It was not only adverse natural conditions which Nicklaus overcame, but personal tragedy as well. On the eve of the tournament he was informed that a close personal friend had been killed in a plane crash while enroute to watch him play. It was only the quiet counsel of his wife, Barbara, that persuaded him to play.

With his victory Nicklaus not only became the first man to successfully defend the Masters title, but also the fourth man to win the Masters title three times.

1970

The final round of the 1970 Masters provided drama of the highest order. Billy Casper, Gene Littler, Gary Player, and Bert Yancey seesawed back and forth in a battle for the lead all day. At one time or another during the round each player either shared the lead or held it all alone.

When the quartet reached the final hole with Yancey and Littler playing just in front of Casper and Player, Casper, Littler, and Player were all tied for the lead with Yancey just one stroke back.

Yancey was eliminated from the hunt when he gambled for a much needed birdie and found the front left greenside bunker with his approach and made bogie. Littler faced an eighteen-footer for birdie and a possible win, but he obviously was playing for a two putt. Casper's approach was marvelous, leaving him just ten feet from victory. When Casper stroked his putt, he knew it was in but the ball stayed out and he remained tied with Littler. Player's end was tragic and typified his week, one in which he was constantly under guard due to threats on his life because of his South African citizenship. His six iron second shot settled near the top lip of the same bunker that had caught Yancey. His explosion still left him eight feet for par and a tie. After backing off once from the putt because of a cameraman, he stepped up and missed to the right. Two Californians were headed to a Monday playoff.

In the playoff Littler was quite untypically off his game while Casper was typically holing putts from every angle. Casper shot 33 on the front nine using only twelve putts while Littler struggled to a 38. But after Casper had extended his lead to seven shots through ten holes, Littler began to slowly chip away. Littler gained a stroke back with a par on twelve, another with a birdie on thirteen, one more with a par on fourteen, and still another with a birdie on fifteen. Quickly the lead was cut to three. But Casper stopped the run with his own birdie on sixteen and finally won the playoff 69 to 74.

The playoff was an interesting struggle between two longtime friends who had played junior golf together in San Diego and were on the same naval base golf team while in the service. Ironically the two had never been involved in a playoff together before.

1979

At times the game of golf can be viciously cruel, preferring to pick its victims at random. Often it selects its victims from the ranks of the kind and gentle. Never was this more true than in the 1979 Masters.

For fifty-four holes the gentle and mild-mannered Ed Sneed had been in complete control of his game and the tournament. Carrying a five-shot margin into the final day, he tenaciously clung to the lead and with three holes remaining still had three shots to spare. Even Fuzzy Zoeller, a first-time Masters participant, who had put on a late charge with birdies on fifteen and seventeen, felt certain he would be relegated to second place.

The pressures of a major championship are often expounded but never exaggerated and Sneed succumbed to the crush over the last three holes. Three-putt greens on the sixteenth and seventeenth left him needing a par to win. His approach to the eighteenth was just wide to the right and his chip was only satisfactory. His par putt refused to fall, dying at the edge of the hole. He stared in disbelief.

Zoeller and Tom Watson had backed into a playoff, the first sudden-death in Masters history.

Beginning at the tenth, Watson nearly ended it, barely missing a birdie putt and all moved to the par-four eleventh. Sneed bunkered his second, but nearly holed his recovery. Zoeller, mercifully, ended Sneed's torment with a short birdie putt after a masterful approach. "The agony of defeat" was never more personified.

Ed Sneed tragically bogied the final three holes of the 1979 Masters and then lost in a playoff to Fuzzy Zoeller.

1982

Sometimes what appears as an almost insurmountable lead can be the most dangerous form of false security. It is often easier to win clinging to a one-shot lead than trying to maintain the status quo with a five- or six-shot margin. Through sixty-three holes the 1982 Masters belonged completely to Craig Stadler. Entering the final nine at Augusta, Stadler held a commanding six-shot lead over four players—Tom Kite, Seve Ballesteros, Tom Weiskopf, and Dan Pohl. No one appeared within striking distance of the mustachioed walrus.

But as he played his way through the back nine, the pressure began to show and shot after shot began to slip away. Unlike before when birdies came easily, now par was the elusive target. A bogie at twelve, the result of a three from the edge, and a fortunate par on thirteen when his second shot jumped the creek and finished on the upward slope of the bank marked the turning point.

Meanwhile Dan Pohl, who was appearing in his first Masters, began to work his way up toward Stadler. Pohl's charge had actually commenced the day before on the back nine when he recorded consecutive eagles on thirteen and fourteen and then followed with birdies on fifteen and sixteen. That amazing stretch had thrust him to within five shots of Stadler.

Playing two holes in front of Stadler on the final day, he began to challenge with birdies on twelve and thirteen, the latter after missing a six-foot eagle putt. But his run was stopped short with a bogie on fourteen and a par on the par-five fifteen after hitting his second shot into the water fronting the green.

He recovered nicely with a birdie on sixteen after his tee shot on the par three stopped just one foot from the hole. Routine pars on the final two holes put him in the clubhouse at 284 (−4).

Meanwhile Stadler was beginning to bleed profusely. He bogied fourteen with a three putt from the back fringe and followed with another at sixteen from the back bunker. He parred seventeen and stood on the seventy-second tee with a one-shot lead. A par would give him the championship. After a perfect tee shot and a second shot to twenty-five feet, there seemed little doubt that the victory was secure. The putt was slightly uphill with little break.

Pressure is defined by Webster as "the burden of physical or mental distress." Golf pressure, whether it be for a two dollar

Craig Stadler at the start of the final round of the 1982 Masters. Stadler played the final nine in four over par 40 to fall into a tie with Dan Pohl whom he defeated on the first sudden-death playoff hole.

nassau or the Masters championship, affects everyone. It encompasses both physical and mental distress. The physiological aspects of pressure are the obvious, the ones that show on the outside of the player. They run the gamut from sweaty palms, to dry mouth, to an increased rapidity of swing pace, and a short, choppy putting stroke.

The psychological aspects, those that drive the sudden physical infirmities, are subtle and sight unseen. The thoughts of "What will the world think of me?" and "What will this mean to my career?" can drive a player to physical failure.

Stadler experienced extreme physical failure on his first putt.

The ball came to rest six feet short of the hole. The second putt was not bold either. It was only adequate, failed to break left as Stadler anticipated, and missed on the right edge of the cup. Stadler stood motionless for what seemed like eternity, shoulders slumped, and heart broken.

There was little solace for the man and there seemed to be no way that he could gird himself up for the playoff to come.

Beginning at the tenth, both players hit satisfactory drives. Stadler played first from the fairway, his ball coming onto the green about thirty-five feet below the hole. Pohl's shot was pushed to the right and the ball finished on the fringe, leaving him a treacherous downhill attempt. Electing to putt the ball, he left the ball about six feet short, still having a downhiller for par. Stadler's putt was sufficient to put the pressure back on Pohl. His first was within eighteen inches and he tapped in for par. Pohl took little time analyzing his putt and the stroke was good but the ball stayed left of the hole and never touched the cup. Stadler had survived a most nightmarish experience in golf.

1987

It is indeed a rare occasion when one spectacular golf shot determines the outcome of a championship; one "miracle" shot that is holed at the opportune time and is forever etched into golf history. Gene Sarazen's albatross at the fifteenth in the 1935 Masters stands out as perhaps the most memorable. But it is seldom, if ever, that such a shot occurs during the course of a playoff. And, until the 1987 Masters, it was a nonexistent species for it had never taken place in a sudden-death playoff for a major championship.

The stunning extra hole triumph of Larry Mize in the 1987 Masters ranks as one of the most storied victories in the history of golf. Born and bred in Augusta, the young Mize had worked the scoreboards at the Masters in exchange for the opportunity to watch the tournament. He could only dream of one day slipping on the green jacket. Only one other player had conquered the golfing world in such dramatic fashion in his own backyard, Francis Ouimet in the 1913 U.S. Open.

Like Ouimet, who defeated the two British giants of the game, Harry Vardon and Ted Ray in the 1913 U.S. Open playoff, Mize defeated the two most formidable stars of the game at that time,

Greg Norman of Australia and Seve Ballesteros of Spain. Like Ouimet, he had figured to be only a bit player to the starring roles of the two foreign players.

Throughout the final round the lead had seesawed back and forth among five or six different players. The eighteenth proved to be the decision point. Mize came in first and produced the needed birdie with a six-foot putt. The Spaniard Ballesteros was next and he saved par from the right, greenside bunker to equal Mize. Finally, came Norman, needing a birdie to win the title outright. His approach finished hole high and just fifteen feet to the right. But his putt for victory agonizingly nicked the edge of the cup and failed to drop.

On the first extra hole Mize had the advantage and barely missed birdie with a fifteen-foot putt, the ball dying to the left just as it approached the hole. Uncharacteristically, Ballesteros three-putted from the right edge of the green for a bogie five and dropped out. Only Mize and Norman continued to the eleventh, the second extra hole.

After both players hit perfect drives, Mize was away for the second shot and badly pushed it to right of the green over one hundred feet from the hole. Norman played safely away from the pond on the left, his shot coming to rest on the right edge of the green some thirty-five feet from the hole.

Now Mize was faced with the seemingly impossible—a delicate pitch to a green that sloped away to water on the far side. Carefully hooding a sand wedge, he gently nursed the ball one-third of the way to the hole and watched as it trickled to the hole and into the hole, dead center.

One man's exuberance is often another man's pain. Norman could only watch in stunned silence. Just seven months earlier he had witnessed Bob Tway hole a bunker shot on the seventy-second hole of the PGA Championship to steal a victory that should have been his. His valiant attempt to tie Mize was hearty but failed.

Once again "David" had triumphed.

1989

If baseball is a game of inches, then golf is a game measured in feet, yards, and often light years. Just ask Scott Hoch. In a tournament complicated by wind, rain, and a wide open scramble for

Greg Norman is the most charismatic figure in the game today. At the same time he is 0 for 3 in major championship playoffs. He lost the 1984 U.S. Open to Fuzzy Zoeller after a dramatic last-round comeback. He lost the 1987 Masters to Larry Mize when Mize holed out from 100 feet on the second playoff hole. And he lost the 1989 British Open to Mark Calcavecchia in a four hole aggregate playoff.

the championship on Sunday, Hoch was bested on the second hole of a sudden-death playoff by Nick Faldo, the 1987 British Open champion. This after he had missed a two-foot putt for par on the first extra hole that would have given him the championship.

When rain canceled the remainder of the third round on Saturday, play resumed in the rain on Sunday with the leader Ben

Crenshaw continuing his third round from the fifteenth hole holding a four-shot lead. But when he finished with a bogie on eighteen, his lead had dwindled to one with twenty-two players within seven shots of the lead.

The 1980 and 1983 Masters champion Seve Ballesteros provided the early fireworks in the final round with a front nine of 31 that included birdies on one, two, four, five, and nine. But a bogie on ten and an ill-fated tee shot into the water on the par-three sixteenth drowned his chances. He finished two back of Faldo and Hoch.

Mike Reid took the lead early on the back nine but he too faded with a three putt on fourteen and a wedge shot that found the water on the par-five fifteenth. He finally finished three strokes out of the playoff.

Greg Norman provided his expected weekend heroics. Following opening rounds of 74 and 75, Norman shot 68 in the third round and went six under for the day on Sunday when he birdied fifteen, sixteen, and seventeen. He now had a share of the lead and all he needed was a par on eighteen to get into the playoff. His five iron approach came up short and he bogied to miss the playoff by one shot.

Throughout the final eighteen holes Crenshaw went up and down the leaderboard. Starting the round with a one-shot lead, he fell back in the early going but regrouped with birdies on the seventieth and seventy-first holes to gain a share of the lead. But strangely he ran out of dry towels in the middle of the eighteenth fairway. On his second shot his grip slipped and the ball fell into the front left bunker. His eight-foot par putt never came close. He too finished one shot back.

Hoch played steady yet unspectacular golf all day and when he birdied the fifteenth to go six under for the tournament, he held a one-stroke lead. That vanished on seventeen when he missed a five-footer for par. He parred eighteen to finish at five under for seventy-two holes and tie Faldo.

But it was Faldo who made the most remarkable move on the final day. Returning to play his final six holes of the third round on Sunday, Faldo played them two over to post a 77 and trail Crenshaw by five. A switch of putters between rounds ignited the Faldo comeback. He birdied one, two, four, and seven on the front nine and finished off the day with birdies on sixteen and seventeen to shoot 65 and tie Hoch at 283 (− 5).

The playoff commenced immediately at the tenth. Daylight was fading fast. Hoch hit the long downhill par four in two, leaving himself thirty feet from the hole. Faldo's four iron second found the right greenside bunker and his explosion left him ten feet for par. Hoch's first putt left him a two-foot downhiller for par. And when the best Faldo could make was a bogie, Hoch began to size up his putt. He sized it up for a full two minutes from every side of the ball. And when he finally got ready to hit it, he stepped away one more time. When the ball finally got going, it never touched the hole. To his credit he made the three-foot uphiller coming back to keep the playoff going. On to the eleventh.

This time the situation reversed itself. Faldo was on the green in two with a twenty-five-footer for birdie while Hoch missed the green to the right. After Hoch pitched to eight feet, Faldo looked over his putt — in reasonable time. The twenty-five-footer went dead center and Faldo reached for the heavens.

Hoch's miss can be simple or difficult to explain. Hoch does have a history of poor putting in pressure situations. In 1987 he three-putted the seventy-second green from eight feet to miss a playoff by one shot. Then there was the fatal missed five-footer at seventeen just a short time before that dropped him out of solo first place. Few putts could ever mean so much. Perhaps the hole looked light years away from the ball. Or perhaps it was because he took light years to line it up and finally hit it. The gremlins of pressure need time to work on the mind. In any case it was a despondent Hoch who met the press: "Right now, I'm glad I don't carry a gun with me."

The victory, of course, pushed Faldo to the top of the golfing world. Adding to his 1987 British Open championship, Faldo had not finished worse than fourth in his last three major championships, including a playoff loss to Curtis Strange in the 1988 U.S. Open. He stood above all the rest in his consistency.

Faldo's success through consistency is a result of his perfectionism. In 1985 he sought the tutelage of golf guru David Ledbetter. For two years Faldo fine-tuned his swing. The ultimate payoff came in the 1987 British Open when he made eighteen straight pars in the final round at Muirfield to overtake American Paul Azinger by one shot. He is one of those rare players who have a true sense of history. When asked the significance of his playoff victory over Hoch, he replied, "That's two."

1990

Déjà vu is not a term commonly associated with golf. Not in a game where course conditions, player variables, and the like differ so drastically from day to day. But for about thirty minutes on April 8, 1990, the tenth and eleventh holes at the Augusta National Golf Club took on an instant replay quality of the 1989 Masters playoff. It was remembered that in 1989 Nick Faldo had defeated Scott Hoch on the second hole of sudden death. In 1990 Nick Faldo defeated Ray Floyd on the second hole of sudden death after the pair had tied at 278 (– 10).

The psychological flashback of the playoff was eerie. As in the 1989 playoff, Faldo hit a poor drive down the right side of the tenth fairway. Then, just as the year before, he followed with a poor second shot into the right greenside bunker. Meanwhile, Floyd was playing the role of Hoch with a good drive and then a seven iron to about fifteen feet below the hole. As in 1989, the end looked like it would come swiftly for Faldo. But thankfully for Faldo the repeat stopped here.

Faldo played his long bunker shot to four feet and then watched as Floyd left his birdie putt six inches short, dead on line with the hole. With a renewed life Faldo made his par putt and the players moved to the eleventh tee.

Enter the twilight zone again.

As in 1989 Faldo played a perfect drive while his opponent was less than ideal from the tee. Floyd played first and struck a solid seven iron but the ball started left of his target. It had no chance to reach the green and fell into the water guarding the left front. Faldo seized the opportunity.

One does not make a mistake and beat Faldo. Paul Azinger, Hoch, and now Floyd have made errors in judgment against Faldo in major championships and all have finished second. Azinger bogied the final two holes of the 1987 British Open and fell by one stroke to Faldo's eighteen straight pars. Hoch missed a two-foot par putt on the first extra hole of the 1989 Masters and lost on the next hole.

Faldo played an eight iron to eighteen feet. The rest, of course, is anticlimatic. Faldo easily made par to successfully defend his Masters championship.

Faldo's victory was a trivia buff's dream. He became only the second player to repeat as champion and coincidentally played

Nick Faldo is the only man to win two playoffs in consecutive years in the same event. Faldo captured the 1989 and 1990 Masters with playoff victories, both on the second extra hole.

with the only other player to successfully defend the Masters title on the final day—Jack Nicklaus. This was also the third time that the defending champion had been involved in a playoff. Faldo followed the likes of Hogan in 1954 and Player in 1962. He was also the first player to win with a female caddy.

Yet, midway through the final round it looked like the quality and quantity of the trivia would be severely depleted. After the ninth hole on the final day Floyd had a three-shot lead and then stretched it to four shots with a twenty-foot birdie putt from behind the twelfth green. With his reputation as a solid front-runner, Floyd looked like a certain winner.

But then Faldo birdied the two par fives, thirteen and fifteen, while Floyd continued to make pars. The lead had dwindled to two.

Faldo cut into the lead again at the sixteenth with a birdie putt from twelve feet on the par three. When Floyd three-putted the seventeenth for bogie, the two were even.

Playing one hole ahead, Faldo carefully two-putted the final hole from the back of the green for par and waited for Floyd. Floyd made the ending dramatic. His tee shot found the first fairway bunker and his second went into the right greenside bunker. He blasted to five feet and coolly sank the putt to preserve the tie. But, despite the final hole dramatics, Floyd could not escape the destiny that had been bestowed on Faldo.

6
U.S. Amateur

There is reasonable conjecture concerning the occurrence of the first U.S. Amateur championship. And depending on your favoritism that conjecture will always remain intact.

In September 1894 a thirty-six hole, stroke play event was conducted at the fashionable Newport Golf Club, Rhode Island. It was four times around the nine hole links in one day. Of the original twenty entries, twelve withdrew during the competition due to the stress and strain. The winner was W. G. Lawrence of Newport who bested the favorite Charles B. Macdonald of Chicago, 188 to 189.

In keeping with his character, Macdonald grumbled and claimed the event was not a true amateur championship inasmuch as it was a stroke play event, not match play which he considered the purest form of amateur competition.

The St. Andrews Golf Club, located just outside of New York City, attempted to indulge the cantankerous Macdonald and invited the competitors to a match play championship in October. Macdonald agreed and smiled just a bit when he extracted a bit of revenge by defeating Lawrence in a semifinal match, 2 and 1. He then prepared to meet L. B. Stoddard of the home club in the final.

The scheduled eighteen hole finale was played in driving rain and Stoddard defeated Macdonald one up after nineteen holes. Macdonald blamed this failure on a party the evening previous to the final that carried on until 5 AM, leaving him in questionable condition to participate in the final.

Macdonald's double defeat quickly escalated a brewing battle between the golf powers of the east and west, which finally culminated in the formation of the United States Golf Association in December 1894. The first official USGA Championships, both open and amateur, were held in October the following year. The amateur event attracted thirty-two players, three of whom defaulted

before their first match. As for Macdonald, he finally won his amateur title, defeating an inexperienced and young Charles E. Sands
in the thirty-six hole final 12 and 11.

Assuming that the first true and legitimate U.S. Amateur
Championship was conducted in 1895 under the auspices of the
United States Golf Association, the tournament was continually
held at match play until 1965 when the USGA decided that a more
worthy champion could be determined under the stroke play format. This format was maintained through 1972 when the USGA
reversed its decision of eight years earlier and reverted back to
match play, a more suitable form of amateur golf they felt.

During the short run of the U.S. Amateur at stroke play, only
one tournament required a playoff to determine the champion. In
accordance with all USGA sponsored events, the playoff was held at
eighteen holes.

1966: Merion Golf Club, Ardmore, Pennsylvania

The play in the 1966 U.S. Amateur could be best described as
erratic, and that leaning more to the errant side than the brilliant.
An exceptionally strong field of amateurs came to Pennsylvania to
challenge the 128 "white faces" of the East Course at Merion. They
left embarrassed and frustrated.

In the end the tournament had to be extended for a playoff in
which Canadian Gary Cowan defeated Deane Beman over eighteen holes 75 to 76 after the pair had tied at 285 in regulation play.
With his victory Cowan became only the third foreign champion
of the U.S. Amateur, following in the footsteps of Englishman
Harold Hilton in 1911 and fellow Canadian Russ Somerville in
1932.

The difficulty of the course and the pressure of the moment
led to a wayward finish, both in regulation play and in the ensuing
playoff.

Playing well in front of Beman on the final day, Cowan was
the only player to overcome the course when he birdied four of the
final seven holes, numbers twelve, fourteen, sixteen, and seventeen. Nevertheless, he still felt he was relegated to second place
when Beman birdied the sixteenth and needed only a bogie-bogie
finish to win.

But in keeping with the overall demeanor of the tournament, Beman collapsed. He bogied the seventeenth after bunkering his tee shot on the 224-yard par three and playing a poor recovery. On the eighteenth, a 457-yard par four, he again bunkered his approach to the green. With a bad lie in the bunker his explosion sailed over the green and his pitch back caught the thick rough and stayed short of the putting surface. He made a valiant chip for the winning five but the ball skidded to the right. The resulting double bogie tied him with Cowan.

Three other players who eventually finished one shot back at 286 also had an opportunity to tie Beman and Cowan. Downing Gray missed a thirty-foot birdie at eighteen and Bob Lewis bogied the final hole, dropping him from the tie.

But none was more bizarre and tragic than what befell Ron Cerrudo. Playing just in front of Beman, Cerrudo missed what he felt was a tying twenty-five-foot birdie putt on the eighteenth. Indifferently he tapped the remaining one-footer with one hand and missed, giving him a bogie and eventually missing the playoff by one stroke. It was an expensive lesson for the young Cerrudo.

The eighteen hole playoff on the following morning took on the resemblance of two men barehandedly passing a hot potato. Neither could accept the responsibility and take charge. Cowan missed six of the first eight fairways but still scrambled to a two over 38 at the turn, tied with Beman, whose game had a bit, but not much more, precision.

Cowan could not accept his good fortune. At number ten he missed a four-footer for birdie to take the lead. On fourteen, while Beman was making bogie for a bunker Cowan three-putted from forty feet to match the bogie. Finally, at fifteen Cowan seized some momentum with the day's first birdie, while Beman bogied after bunkering his tee shot.

But as quickly as the momentum shifted to Cowan, he squelched it. After pulling his tee shot into a fairway bunker on sixteen, he elected to go for the green. The decision was disastrous. The ball caught the top lip of the bunker and landed in the tall grass of the quarry. His third was long, a chip for his fourth came up short, and he finally posted a triple-bogie seven. Beman, however, could still not seize the lead. He bogied the hole and the pair went to the seventeenth all even.

At the seventeenth the untimely again occurred. Cowan faced a slippery thirty-footer for birdie, while Beman was about fifteen feet for birdie. Cowan made a tidy two putt, but Beman, whose strength was in his putting, three-putted, missing the second putt from three feet.

But still the drama was not complete. Beman reached the eighteenth in two with a driver and a four wood, while Cowan's second carried him a yard or so over the green. The pressure squeezed Cowan and he left his chip nine feet short. Beman went for his birdie and missed, leaving six feet coming back. He boldly made the par. Now Cowan had the "hot potato." His putt was firm and dead center all the way, giving him a merciful one-stroke victory and the title.

Part II. WOMEN

7
Introduction

While women's golf has always lagged behind the men's game in terms of participation, the enthusiasm of the ladies for the game has always been on an equal plane. The first dedicated woman golfer was credited to be Mary Queen of Scots, who frequently forsook her regal duties to enjoy a few holes of golf. So enthralled was she with the game that in 1567 she was spotted on the links just three days after her husband's murder.

She was, however, very much a loner in a male only sport. It was not until some three hundred years later that women were again conspicuous on the golf course, this time over the links at Musselburgh in Scotland. Inevitably, in 1867 the first women's club was begun at St. Andrews, Scotland, and the game immediately began to increase in popularity with women.

The first formal organization for women was the Ladies' Golf Union formed in Great Britain in 1893. The creation of the LGU signaled the beginning of organized competition for ladies with the inaugural British Ladies' Championship that same year. The first women's competition in the United States took place in 1895 with the U.S. Women's Championship at the Meadowbrook Club in Hempstead, New York.

With the inception of competition the quality of women's golf increased rapidly on both sides of the Atlantic with top-notch players like Dorothy Campbell Hurd, Cecil Leitch, the incomparable Glenna Collett Vare, and Joyce Wethered.

Finally in 1940 came Patty Berg and Babe Didrikson Zaharias, an Olympic legend who had turned her athletic endeavors to golf. Once again the caliber of women's golf was raised to new heights.

In 1944 Hope Seignious, a professional from North Carolina, formed the Women's Professional Golf Association, but the fledgling organization disintegrated just over three years later, mainly due to a lack of quality play outside of a few.

However, in 1950 with the help of Wilson Sporting Goods and under the guidance of Fred Corcoran, who was at the time managing the career of Zaharias, the organization was resurrected as the Ladies Professional Golf Association. Gradually, but with intense growing pains, the organization grew, due chiefly to the presence of Zaharias, Berg, and Louise Suggs. From an initial beginning of seven tournaments in 1950, the ladies of the LPGA can today participate in over thirty-five events a year.

Against this backdrop the major championships evolved. Beginning in 1937 the Titleholders Championship and the Western Open were the only events considered as major championships. When the Titleholders was suspended from 1943–45, The Western Open continued as the sole major championship.

In 1946 the Titleholders was resumed and the U.S. Open was inaugurated, giving the ladies three major championship competitions. These three events remained intact until 1955 when the LPGA Championship was instituted, bringing the total to four.

The four majors remained constant until 1967 when the Titleholders was once again suspended. The following year the Western Open faded from the scene and reduced the number of majors to two once again. In 1972 the Titleholders was played one last time, bringing three majors to that year.

In 1979 the du Maurier Classic was elevated to major championship status after a six-year run as a regular LPGA Tour event. Once more the total of major championships was three. Eventually the total again reached the magic number of four in 1983 when the Nabisco Dinah Shore was officially designated as a major championship. Today these same four tournaments, the LPGA championship, the U.S. Open, the du Maurier Classic, and the Nabisco Dinah Shore, are the designated major championships for women.

Within the six tournaments that have been considered major championships, there have been fourteen ties after regulation play and a resulting playoff. Each of the six majors has played host to at least one playoff. The U.S. Open has witnessed the most playoffs in women's major championship golf with six. Next follows the LPGA with three. Only one playoff has involved more than two players—the 1987 playoff for the U.S. Open which encompassed three.

8
Women's Western Open

The Women's Western Open holds a premier position in the history of women's professional golf. The Women's Western Golf Association began the Western Amateur in 1901 and then followed in 1930 with the Western Open, a tournament for ladies from public and daily fee courses. In 1935 Helen Hicks and Babe Didrikson, two professionals, were admitted to the field. This was the first event in which female professionals and amateurs competed in the same event. The first year for a monetary purse was 1941 with Patty Berg winning $100 for first place. The tournament continued until 1967. Of the thirty-three tournaments conducted during that span only one playoff was required to determine a winner.

1960: Beverly Country Club, Chicago, Illinois

In 1960 the Beverly Country Club hosted the Women's Western Open. Playing to a par of 73, the course proved to be a severe test for the championship.

Betsy Rawls led going into the final round but fired an 81 and finished at 306. Eventually, Joyce Ziske and Barbara Romack tied at 301 (+ 9).

In the sudden-death playoff Ziske parred the par-five second extra hole to defeat Romack.

9
Titleholders

The Women's Titleholders Championship was one of the first professional events conducted for women. The tournament was sponsored by the Titleholders Golf Association and run by Eileen Stulb. It began in 1937 and continued for thirty years to 1966 with the exception of the years 1943–45 due to the war.

The tournament was reinstituted for one additional year in 1972 at the Pine Needles Golf Club in Pinehurst, North Carolina, under the direction of Warren Bell whose wife, Peggy Kirk Bell, was the only amateur champion of the event.

The championship was held annually, usually in March, at the Augusta Country Club in Augusta, Georgia, the next-door neighbor to the Augusta National Golf Club. The course played to a par of 72 and measured 6,300 yards. Of the twenty-seven tournaments conducted at the Augusta Country Club, only one required a play-off.

1962

In 1962 Mickey Wright had reached the pinnacle of her career. Since joining the LPGA tour in 1956, she had amassed thirty victories that included three major championships in 1961, the LPGA Championship, the U.S. Women's Open, and the Titleholders. The Grand Slam eluded her when she finished second in the Women's Western Open.

The twenty-third renewal of the Titleholders at the Augusta Country Club included a field of thirty professionals and nineteen amateurs. On the final day of regulation play no less than six players had the opportunity to win the championship. Barbara Romack needed a birdie three on the final hole to tie, but she failed to hole a chip and eventually settled for a bogie five and a 297 total.

Wright arrived at the final green needing to get down in two from the edge of the green for a tie. After a somewhat poor chip, she sank a ten-footer for par and a total of 295 (+7). The heroics of Ruth Jessen on the final hole were even more impressive. After badly hooking her drive, she played a spectacular recovery to the green, threading the ball over and between trees with a five iron. The par four tied her with Wright.

In the playoff Wright was unbeatable. She recorded nines of 34 and 35 for a three under par 69 and a three-shot victory over Jessen. Wright's 69 was also the lowest round of the tournament.

With her victory Wright became the first player since 1942 to successfully defend the Titleholders Championship.

10
U.S. Women's Open

The queen of all women's major championship tournaments is the United States Women's Open. It is the oldest continuing major championship for women professional golfers. At its inception in 1946 as a match play event, it was conducted by the Women's Professional Golfer's Association under the guidance of Hope Segnious. In 1949 the Ladies' PGA assumed administration of the tournament under the advisement of Fred Corcoran. Finally in 1953 the United States Golf Association took charge and continues to be the administrative agency.

Following a single year term as a match play tournament, the championship converted to stroke play in 1947 and has remained as such to the present time. In 1965 when the men's event switched to four days of play, the women's championship followed suit. Of the forty-two championships conducted at stroke play, six have required a playoff to determine the champion. In keeping with USGA policy and tradition, each playoff, beginning with the first in 1953, has been held at eighteen holes.

Like the men's championship, the USGA decided to move the site for the championship to a different course each year. While the tournament has always been played on adequate courses, as women's play has become more popular and has improved in quality, the championship in recent years has been conducted on top quality courses such as the Hazeltine National Golf Club in 1970, the Baltusrol Golf Club in 1985, and the Atlanta Athletic Club in 1990. The 1991 tournament is scheduled to be played at the Colonial Country Club.

1953: Country Club of Rochester, Rochester, New York

The initial U.S. Women's Open administered by the USGA drew thirty-eight entries at the historic Country Club of Rochester. The field represented the best in women's golf. The event was conducted in the same manner as the men's open with eighteen holes on Thursday, eighteen holes on Friday, and a thirty-six hole finale on Saturday.

The Country Club of Rochester was established in 1895. Its most famous son is the flamboyant Walter Hagen, who served in a professional capacity there before conquering the world of professional golf. The course for the 1953 ladies' tournament was stretched to a demanding 6,417 yards, par 74, with virtually no holes being of the pitch-and-putt variety.

After seventy-two holes of regulation play two players remained tied at 302, Betsy Rawls, the fifth player inducted into the LPGA Hall of Fame in 1960 and a Chinese-Hawaiian player named Jackie Pung.

However, from the outset of the tournament it appeared that Patty Berg would run away with the tournament. She led by eight strokes after thirty-six holes and three after fifty-four. And even with three holes remaining she still maintained a two-shot advantage. However, the difficulty of the course led to her demise and she finished one stroke back of Rawls and Pung with a bogie-bogie-bogie finish over the final three holes.

Pung herself had an opportunity to win the tournament outright but she too bogied the final hole and finished the day with an even par round of 74 and a 302 total.

In comparison, Rawls was the only player in contention who could contend with the final three holes finishing par, par, par, the one on the last hole coming with a two putt from sixty feet.

In the eighteen hole playoff the next day, Rawls played brilliant and in effect unbeatable golf, firing a three under par 71 that featured a front nine of 34. While Pung played respectably, she was no match for the nearly perfect game that Rawls produced. The final was Rawls 71, Pung 77.

For Pung it was surely a disappointment to have lost, but sadly nothing in comparison with the tragedy that befell her four years later in the Open. She remains to this day, along with the

Argentinian Roberto De Vicenzo, one of the two most tragic figures in the annals of major championship golf.

Having played spectacular and popular golf in the 1957 U.S. Women's Open at Winged Foot, Pung appeared to be the winner. However, forty minutes after she had apparently secured victory, it was announced that she had signed an incorrect scorecard and had been disqualified. In error she had signed for a "5" on the fourth hole, not the "6" she had played to. The penalty for signing for a score lower than actually received is disqualification. The literal rule of the game had been breached and its honor upheld, but the countenance on the face of the game had fallen.

Betsy Rawls's commitment, dedication, and service to the game of golf cannot be understated. Her 1953 victory was the second of four U.S. Women's Open titles. She also captured four other major championships. Her total of fifty-five career victories places her behind only Kathy Whitworth, Mickey Wright, and Patty Berg on the all-time list. A Phi Beta Kappa graduate from the University of Texas, she has a masterful command of the rules of golf and was the first woman to serve on the Rules Committee for the men's U.S. Open. After retiring from competition in 1975, she served as the LPGA's tournament director for six years. In 1981 she left that position to become the executive director of the McDonald's Championship, a position she still holds today.

1956: Northland Country Club, Duluth, Minnestoa

In 1956 the U.S. Women's Open came to the northernmost confines of the United Sates. The Northland Country Club in Duluth, Minnesota, is one of the many Donald Ross layouts that he produced during the early part of the century. Curiously, Ross was so busy that he himself urged the membership to accept the design of another architect. They would not be denied, however, and persisted in having a Donald Ross-designed golf course. The spectacular views of Lake Superior combined with a Ross design lined with evergreens on virtually every hole provided a stern test for the women professionals and amateurs.

And after seventy-two holes of regulation play there was one professional and one amateur that remained tied for the championship. Kathy Cornelius, a first-year professional and mother of a two-year-old, and Barbara McIntire, a twenty-one-year-old amateur, tied at 302. McIntire still remains the only female amateur to be involved in a playoff for a major championship.

The final hole of regulation, a 410-yard par five, provided the drama. McIntire made a thirty-foot eagle putt to finish at 302. Her comeback over the last eighteen holes was spectacular. Beginning the final day eight strokes behind coleaders Cornelius and Hagge, McIntire finished 3–3–3, birdie, par, eagle, to gain a tie for the championship.

Moments later Patty Berg barely missed a twenty-foot eagle that would have tied her with McIntire. Finally came Cornelius and Marlene Hagge. The pair had been trading the lead for most of the day but as they came up the seventy-second, Cornelius led Hagge by two and needed only a par for 301 to secure the victory. Electing to play safely and lay up short of the creek in front of the green, Cornelius was stunned when her lay-up shot trickled into the water. A bogie was the best she could do and her total of 302 tied her with McIntire. Meanwhile, Hagge was green high in two and chipped her third shot to six feet. But her tying birdie putt skidded by and she finished tied with Berg at 303.

Despite her disheartening finish of the previous day, Cornelius never trailed in the playoff. McIntire struggled all day and could not keep pace with the consistent Cornelius. At the eighth Cornelius began to steadily pull away. She gained one at the eighth, one at the eleventh, one at the twelfth, and one more at the thirteenth. When they had finished, Cornelius had won the playoff 75 to 82.

1964: San Diego Country Club, Chula Vista, California

In 1964 the USGA moved the Women's Open Championship to the west coast. Originating in 1897, the San Diego Country Club played to a yardage of 6,376 and a par of 73. It was characterized by narrow fairways and huge greens.

From the outset of the tournament it appeared that Mickey Wright, a former member of the club, was destined to win the title. She was the leader or tied for the lead at the end of every round. However, at the end of seventy-two holes she found herself tied with Ruth Jessen at 290 (– 2). The pair had previously squared off in a playoff for the 1962 Titleholders Championship.

Gaining that tie did not come easily for Wright. Coming to the seventy-second hole Jessen trailed Wright by one shot. She fired her five wood second shot on the par four to within two feet and made birdie. At the same time Wright bunkered her second shot, but played a magnificent trap shot to three feet and made the putt to preserve the tie.

In the playoff Wright took the lead on the sixth with a birdie two and never relinquished it. Her steady play eventually wore down the scrambling Jessen who hit only six greens in regulation during the playoff. Wright won the head-to-head duel 70 to 72.

Mickey Wright is truly one of the legends of the game, male or female. Her statistics are astounding. With eighty-two professional victories she is second only to Kathy Whitworth. Between 1959 and 1968 she amassed seventy-nine professional victories. Her most prolific year was 1961 when she captured three of the four women's major championsips, U.S. Women's Open, the LPGA Championship, and the Titleholders Championship. Many golf swing experts have credited her with the perfect swing. Much like Hogan, she was a masterful technician with the golf swing both in application and theory.

1976: Rolling Green Country Club, Springfield, Pennsylvania

In the 1976 U.S. Women's Open the Rolling Green Country Club proved that short does not equal easy. As set up for the tournament the course measured 6,066 yards with a par of 71. It was the shortest in U.S. Open history up to that time. Yet, despite its limited length, the course was playing diabolically. Additionally, rainy weather prior to and during the tournament made the conditions even more difficult. Rain on Sunday morning caused a delay in the start and forced the USGA to go to split-tees for the day.

Eventually, the course sorted out two players to enter an extra eighteen holes on the following Monday, JoAnne Carner and Sandra Palmer, both tying at 292 (+ 8).

The rain delay on the final day of regulation play only heightened the tension and the drama. Beginning the last round,

Carner trailed Palmer by two shots with Jane Blalock another shot back. As Blalock faded Carner and Palmer staged an up and down battle throughout the day with the climax finally coming on the seventy-second hole. Playing in front of Palmer, Carner made a tidy par on the last and waited. It finally came down to a six-foot downhiller for Palmer to tie. The putt was dead center and they headed to Monday.

Carner jumped out early on Monday with a birdie on the first hole and held a two-stroke margin after nine, despite two bogies. After gaining one stroke back on the tenth, Palmer gave three back with bogies on eleven, twelve, and thirteen. With a four-stroke lead and five holes to play it looked like a certain victory for Carner. But then she lost control of her game and went double bogie, bogie, bogie, while Palmer went 3–3–3 to gain a one-shot advantage.

But Carner has bulldog determination and she rebounded with a birdie at the par-five seventeenth while Palmer made six after hooking her second shot into a bunker.

On the par-five eighteenth, with a strong breeze blowing, Carner was left in the trees off the tee, but Palmer's tee shot hit a tree and stopped eighty yards off the tee. The best she could do was six. Carner recovered to the fairway and, despite a poor pitch to sixty feet, two-putted for par and a two-shot victory, 76 to 78.

This playoff victory was Carner's second U.S. Open Championship. She had previously captured the title in 1971. Carner has also compiled one of the greatest records in USGA history. In addition to her two U.S. Open victories, she has won five U.S. Amateur titles (1957, 1960, 1962, 1966, and 1968) and the U.S. Girls Junior (1956). She is the only player to hold those three titles. She was inducted into the LPGA Hall of Fame in 1982 and the World Golf Hall of Fame in 1985.

1986: NCR Golf Course, Dayton, Ohio

The first victory in a player's professional career is one that is certainly remembered. And when that victory is the most prestigious prize in women's golf, the victory can be sweeter than life itself.

Such was the case for twenty-six-year-old Jane Geddes who overcame not only an eighteen hole playoff, but also a tournament complicated by manmade and natural disasters.

In a week that saw a phosphorus tank fire caused by a forty-four-car train derailment, a Saturday morning earthquake that measured 4.2 on the Richter scale, and violent thunderstorms that delayed play on the first three days of the tournament, Geddes prevailed in an eighteen hole playoff over Sally Little after the pair had tied over 72 holes at 287 (−1).

The South Course of the NCR Country Club, also the site of the 1969 PGA Championship, is a hilly layout carved from hardwood forests that are characteristic of the locale. The course was designed by Louis Sibbett Wilson and opened for play in 1954. It provided another excellent test for the U.S. Women's Open.

Over the last nine holes on the final day of regulation play, four players had the opportunity to either win the title outright or gain a tie. Geddes made the first move, charging from behind with birdies on twelve, fourteen, and seventeen. And when she parred eighteen, she was safely in at 287 (−1). Little was next, coming to the final hole needing a birdie to win. Her thirty-foot birdie putt stopped just inches short and tap-in par tied her with Geddes. Finally the third round leaders Betsy King and Ayako Okamoto failed on birdie putts at the eighteenth that would have gained them a tie for the championship. In the end only Geddes and Little had survived a wild and earthshaking week.

In the playoff Little started fast with three straight birdies on four, five, and six and leaped to a three-shot lead. But she quickly gave her margin back plus one when she bogied the eighth and double bogied the ninth while Geddes was making a birdie and a par on the same.

Little evened the seesaw match again at the tenth with a birdie. At last, one lady grabbed the momentum for good. It was Geddes, who at the thirteenth gallantly saved par from off the green and watched as Little lipped out a fifteen-foot birdie putt. She then took the advantage with a birdie at fourteen and added another stroke with a par three at fifteen when Little bogied. The two-stroke margin remained until the end. The ordeal had ended, Geddes had won 71 to 73 for her first professional victory as well as her first major championship.

It was a remarkable victory for Geddes, who began the game at the advanced age of seventeen. Incredibly, two years later she qualified for match play in the Women's Amateur, although she lost in the first round. In 1983 she turned professional and, despite consistent play, had not won until this tournament. With her win she followed in the footsteps of Kathy Baker, who likewise made the U.S. Women's Open her first professional victory in 1985.

Little's loss in the playoff stymied a courageous comeback attempt by the native South African. After fourteen victories in seven years on the LPGA Tour, highlighted by 1971 LPGA Rookie of the Year honors and a victory in the Women's Internatinal where she holed an eighty-foot bunker shot for a birdie on the final hole, her career was stopped short in 1982 by abdominal surgery and recurring knee problems that required arthroscopic surgery. She had not won since that time and was struggling to regain her health and previous form.

1987: Plainfield Country Club, Plainfield, New Jersey

The first and only three-way playoff for the U.S. Women's Open Championship featured a formidable international cast that included Laura Davies of Great Britain, Ayako Okamoto of Japan, and JoAnne Carner of the United States, three players with equal talent but diverse games.

Davies's is one of power. Her booming drives often give her the option of going for most par fives in two. Surprisingly, she also has a deft touch around the greens. Okamoto is a master technician, who relies on a game of finesse. Carner possesses a compact swing that delivers surprising power and length. Her iron shots are characterized by a low, boring trajectory and extreme accuracy.

Despite the thrilling finish and the tense playoff, for the second year in a row the tournament was again overshadowed by the elements. The event, which was plagued by intense heat with temperatures in the 90s and heavy rains, required six days to complete with the eighteen hole playoff finally being held on Tuesday.

The weather conditions became so bad on Sunday that before the leaders could tee off for their final round, a quick storm dumped two inches of rain on the course and rendered it unplayable. Wisely, the USGA decided to call it a day and postponed the remainder of the final round until Monday.

When the final round eventually did get underway, Okamoto, still seeking her first major victory, jumped out to a three-stroke advantage after eight holes. But she quickly gave her advantage back when she four-putted the ninth green to fall into a tie with Davies.

The final turning point for Okamoto came on the thirteenth green. Faced with a four-foot, downhill, left-to-right breaking putt for birdie, she was stymied by a spike mark straight on her intended line. In an attempt to maneuver the ball around the mark, she hit the first putt three feet past and missed the return for par.

Carner gave the patriotic American fans reason for celebration with birdies on fifteen and seventeen that vaulted her to a one-stroke lead heading to the eighteenth. Then she too fell back with a three putt from the collar of the final green.

Neither Davies nor Okamoto were able to capitalize on Carner's mistake and all three finished the tournament at 285 (– 3), setting up the first three-way playoff of the championship.

Tuesday's eighteen hole playoff was a seesaw affair from the start. Each woman either held the lead outright or possessed a share of it at various times. The long-hitting Davies drew first blood with a birdie on the fourth. When Okamoto bogied the fifth and sixth and Carner likewise the sixth and seventh, Davies jumped to a two-shot advantage, despite her own bogie at seven.

A birdie by Carner on nine coupled with a bogie by Davies on ten put the two even, now just one ahead of Okamoto. Something had to give and it did over the next five holes.

Carner bogied the eleventh and thirteenth to fall two behind Davies and one behind Okamoto. Davies then provided the final blows to her adversaries with a twenty-foot birdie on fourteen and a thirty-five footer on fifteen. Despite birdies by Carner and Okamoto on sixteen, Davies held on with pars over the final three holes to win by two over Okamoto and three over Carner. The final scores were Davies 71, Okamoto 73, and Carner 74.

For Okamoto, who did not begin the sport until the age of twenty-four, it was another bitter disappointment in her quest for a major championship, an accomplishment that would elevate her to the top of the profession.

With her victory, the twenty-three-year-old Englishwoman, who was playing in only her third major championship in the United States, became the first woman from Great Britain and only the fourth foreign champion of the event. She followed Fay Crocker of Uruguay (1955), the amateur Catherine Lacoste of France (1967), and Jan Stephenson of Australia (1983). And like the two previous U.S. Women's Open champions, the victory was her first on U.S. soil. She also became the first to hold both the U.S. and British Women's Open championships simultaneously.

11
LPGA Championship

The LPGA Championship which began in 1955 has always been conducted as a seventy-two hole stroke play event with the exception of its inaugural year when it employed the unusual format of fifty-four holes of stroke play followed by a match play final between the top two finishers. In its thirty-five-year history, only three of the championships have required a playoff following regulation play. The first tie in 1956 was decided by a sudden-death playoff and the two following were resolved over eighteen holes.

While there have been brief periods when the event has been held at various courses, the venue for the tournament has traditionally remained at the same course for several years. From 1961 to 1966 the Stardust Country Club in Las Vegas, Nevada, played host to the championship. In 1967 the event moved to Pleasant Valley Country Club in Sutton, Massachusetts, and remained there through 1974, with the exception of 1969. Most recently, the Jack Nicklaus Golf Course at King's Island, Ohio, has been the home for the tournament.

1956: Forest Lake Country Club, Detroit, Michigan

It is fitting that the first playoff in a women's major championship would be contested between two of the founding and charter members of the LPGA, Marlene Hagge and Patty Berg. In just the second year of the championship Hagge and Berg tied at the end of seventy-two holes with scores of 291. The tournament itself marked a milestone for the LPGA with twenty-five professional entries, the largest for any LPGA tournament up to that time.

In the final round of regulation play it appeared that the tournament was Berg's to win or lose. However, she faded over the last three holes finishing with 5-5-5 while Hagge played them in 4-4-5 to gain a tie.

On the first hole of the sudden death playoff, a 490-yard par five, both players were on the fringe in three. Berg chipped first, the ball finishing seven feet short of the hole. Hagge's chip stopped just eighteen inches away. When Berg missed her par putt, Hagge tapped in for the win. The victory was Hagge's third consecutive LPGA triumph.

Marlene Hagge's professional career began in 1950 at the age of sixteen when she became a charter and founding member of the LPGA. She has been competing on the tour ever since. Her first victory came in 1952 at the age of eighteen and she remains the youngest LPGA winner.

When one speaks of legends in the game of golf the name of Patty Berg is always mentioned. She is credited with fifty-seven victories since turning professional in 1940. Forty-four of those victories were on the LPGA tour. She has amassed fifteen major championships, including seven Western Opens, seven Titleholders, and one U.S. Open.

1968: Pleasant Valley Country Club, Sutton, Massachusetts

In 1968 the LPGA Championship returned to the Pleasant Valley Country Club for the second consecutive year. The course is set in the apple orchards of central Massachusetts and features huge greens and hilly terrain where seldom is found a level lie. The layout measures 6,130 yards and plays to a par of 73. The 1968 tournament was also affected by the wind, which made putting on the large greens a most challenging task.

When the regulation seventy-two holes had been completed, Sandra Post, a twenty-year-old tour rookie from Canada and Kathy Whitworth, already the holder of four major championships and the defending champion in this event, tied at 294 (+2).

Beginning the final day of regulation play Post and Whitworth were deadlocked at 221 for the fifty-four holes. But surprisingly the rookie Post played steady throughout the day and when Whitworth came to the seventy-second hole, she was forced to hole a three-foot birdie putt to tie for the championship.

On the next day in the first eighteen hole playoff to decide the LPGA Championship, Post easily defeated Whitworth 68 to 75. During the course of the playoff both Post and Whitworth played well but it was Post's ability to get the ball in from seemingly everywhere that proved to be the difference.

With her victory Post became the first rookie to win an LPGA event since 1961 and the youngest winner of a women's major championship.

1970: Pleasant Valley Country Club, Sutton, Massachusetts

In 1970 the LPGA Championship returned to the hills of central Massachusetts for the third time in four years after a one-year stop at the Concord Golf Club in Kiameshia Lake, New York. And, as in the previous visit to Pleasant Valley in 1968, two players remained tied at the top at the end of the regulation seventy-two holes. Shirley Englehorn and Kathy Whitworth, a participant in the 1968 playoff, tied at 285 (−7).

Once again the par-five seventy-second hole was the stage for some heroics and dramatics. Englehorn birdied the long uphill dogleg afer hitting a wedge to twelve inches on her third shot. Whitworth came to the final hole needing a birdie to win and barely missed a fifteen-footer for the title.

In the eighteen hole playoff the play was somewhat unspectacular. Whitworth uncharacteristically lost patience, claiming in later years that it seemed like it took forever to play the round. In the end Englehorn won the playoff 74 to 78.

With her victory Englehorn capped a courageous comeback from a horseback riding accident and a severe ankle injury received in an automobile accident.

For Whitworth it was her second consecutive playoff loss at the Pleasant Valley course. Nevertheless, her golfing achievements are legendary. With eighty-eight career professional victories she is the winningest professional golfer of all time, male or female. On the LPGA Tour she was the leading money winner eight times, Player of the Year seven times, and the Vare Trophy winner seven times. She was inducted into the LPGA Hall of Fame in 1975. She is the winner of six major championships, including three LPGA Championships, two Titleholders, and one Western Open. Yet, like Sam Snead on the men's side, Whitworth remains one of the great enigmas of the sport. She has never won the U.S. Open. And what makes the situation even more difficult to understand is the fact that the event was played on several courses that she had won on previously.

12
Nabisco Dinah Shore

The Nabisco Dinah Shore Championship is the one major championship for women which has continually been played over the same course since its inception, the Mission Hills Country Club in Rancho Mirage, California.

Although inaugurated in 1972 as the Colgate Dinah Shore, it has only been since 1983 that the event has enjoyed designation as a major championship. Since its elevation to major championship status, two playoffs have been required to determine the champion. Both have been conducted under the sudden-death format.

The Mission Hills Country Club is a severe test for the LPGA golfers. It is long by average LPGA standards, measuring over 6,200 yards and playing to a par of 36–36–72. Typical of its difficulty is the par-four thirteenth which plays uphill to a yardage of 380, with the prevailing wind always in the player's face. But the greatest challenge of the course is the wind which can alter a player's distance by as much as three clubs.

1984

In only its second year as a major championship, the Nabisco Dinah Shore experienced its first playoff to determine the champion. The combatants made for an interesting contrast. Juli Inkster, a three-time U.S. Amateur champion but a rookie on the LPGA Tour, and Pat Bradley, a ten-year veteran with thirteen victories, including the 1980 du Maurier Classic and the 1981 U.S. Open. The pair had tied at 280 (– 8).

The rookie had shown her determination with a final round 68 that featured a birdie on the final hole to gain the tie with Bradley.

The sudden-death playoff which started at the par-four

fifteenth, which requires extreme accuracy from the tee, came to a quick and shocking conclusion. After Bradley had driven safely from the tee, Inkster mistakenly had the driver in her hand. Too nervous to exchange it for a three wood, she blasted the tee shot perfectly down the middle. Her second shot with an eight iron was safely on twenty feet from the cup. Inkster won sudden-death play-off 4 to 5.

For Inkster, a three-time U.S. Amateur champion, the victory was her first in a major event as a professional, even at the young age of twenty-three. But she did not stop there. In her last event as a rookie, she shot a final round 67 to win the du Maurier Classic and became the first rookie ever to win two major championships in her rookie season.

The arrival of Juli Inkster to the LPGA Tour was much awaited. With three consecutive victories in the U.S. Amateur from 1980–82 all the experts predicted LPGA stardom for Inkster. But in her first attempt to qualify for the tour she failed and she seriously considered giving up professional golf. Fortunately her husband encouraged her and she qualified on her next attempt.

1987

In the 1987 Nabisco Dinah Shore Betsy King finally accomplished what she and others had been expecting for a long time, a victory in a major championship. Although she had collected eight victories since joining the LPGA tour in 1984, she had yet to win a major championship.

But her first victory in a major championship did not come easily. In the second round she had to endure stiff winds that gusted up to forty mph. In the final round she had to overcome a charge by Patty Sheehan that produced a seven under par 65 which featured eight birdies and a lone bogie.

The final round of the seventy-two hole event produced pressure golf at its best. Playing two groups in front of coleaders King and Pat Bradley, Sheehan had three shots to make up. She began her comeback immediately with three straight birdies, only to be duplicated by King. Sheehan followed with another birdie at six. Meanwhile, Bradley birdied the fifth and eighth. The three began the final nine with just two shots separating them—Sheehan two under, Bradley three under, and King four under.

Sheehan completed her charge with birdies at ten and eleven and Bradley remained even with her own birdie at ten. King then regained the lead with a birdie at twelve while Bradley stumbled with a bogie. Sheehan deadlocked King again at fourteen with her seventh birdie in fourteen holes.

Finally, King and Sheehan slipped. King bogied the thirteenth and Sheehan the fifteenth while Bradley birdied the thirteenth. They headed to the sixteenth tee all even at four under. The dramatics were yet to come.

Sheehan birdied the par-four sixteenth after punching a six iron under a tree to fifteen feet. King answered in dramatic style. After pulling her drive left and then pushing her second into the right greenside bunker, King holed the forty-five-foot trap shot to stay even with Sheehan. It was one of the most dramatic shots in a major championship and certainly the deciding shot of the tournament.

All three parred their remaining holes with Sheehan just missing her birdie attempt at the last. Only two, King and Sheehan, were left at 283 (– 5) and headed for sudden-death.

On the first hole of sudden-death, the narrow par four fifteenth, King again displayed her skillful shot making. After pushing her drive behind some trees and chipping back to the fairway, she hit a 100-yard wedge to five feet and saved par to tie Sheehan.

An unexpected finish came at the sixteenth, the site of King's dramatics just moments earlier. With both players lying two on the green about twenty feet away, Sheehan putted first and came up three feet short. King putted to two and one half feet and marked. When Sheehan's putt skidded to the right of the hole, King seized the opportunity and holed the putt to win her first major championship.

King's victory was merely the stepping-stone to superstar status. In 1989 she set an LPGA record for earnings in a single season with $654,132. The season included six titles, highlighted by a victory in the U.S. Open. In 1990 she added two more major championships when she again won the Dinah Shore and then successfully defended her championship in the U.S. Open.

13
du Maurier Classic

Like the Nabisco Dinah Shore, the du Maurier Classic is another of the women's major championships that has evolved to such status only in recent years. Inaugurated in 1973 as the La Canadienne and conducted as the Peter Jackson Classic from 1974–82, the event became the du Maurier Classic in 1983. During its designation as the Peter Jackson Classic, it officially attained major championship status in 1979.

The tournament is annually played in Canada and changes its venue each year within that country. Of the ten tournaments conducted under major championship status, only one has resulted in a tie at the end of regulation play. All ties for the championship are resolved in a sudden-death playoff.

1986: Board of Trade Country Club, Toronto, Canada

Twenty years had passed since a woman had won three major championships in a single season. The feat had previously been accomplished in 1961 when Mickey Wright won the LPGA Championship, the U.S. Open, and the Titleholders, a now defunct major. All that changed in 1986 when Pat Bradley completed the triple with a sudden-death victory in the du Maurier Classic over Japan's Ayako Okamoto after the pair had tied at 276 (– 12) over seventy-two holes.

The venue for the tournament was the West Course of the Board of Trade Country Club in Toronto, Canada, a hilly layout that demands stamina as well as exact shot making.

The victory capped a most impressive year for Bradley and elevated her from the status of great player to superstar. The victory

134

also enabled her to successfully defend the title she had won in 1985 and, together with her victory in 1980, made her the first three-time winner of the event.

Capturing the title did not come easily, however. Although she recorded a final round 66, she could do no better than tie Okamoto who closed with a spectacular 64.

While neither Bradley nor Okamoto held the third round lead—that distinction went to Chris Johnson—the final round quickly emerged into a match play contest between the two.

Bradley promptly began the final eighteen with birdies on five of the first six holes. Meanwhile, Okamoto was making five birdies of her own on the outward half to stay hot on Bradley's heels.

The lead seesawed through the back nine and when Bradley came to the final hole, she still needed a birdie to tie Okamoto. After hitting her second on the par five to the side of the green, she was faced with a difficult lie and a precarious pin placement. She played a deft chip to six feet and coolly holed the putt to force the playoff.

In the playoff which began at the par-three sixteenth, Bradley hit first and struck a splendid six iron to ten feet under the hole. Okamoto answered with a superb shot of her own to twelve feet above the hole. When Okamoto missed her birdie attempt, Bradley left no doubt, firmly holing her putt into the dead center for a birdie two and the victory.

Appendix 1: Men

Chronological Playoff Listing

Year	Tournament	Winner	Runner-Up
1876	British Open	Martin, Robert	Strath, David
1883	British Open	Fernie, Willie	Ferguson, Robert
1889	British Open	Park, Willie, Jr.	Kirkaldy, Andrew
1896	British Open	Vardon, Harry	Taylor, John H.
1901	U.S. Open	Anderson, Willie	Smith, Alex
1903	U.S. Open	Anderson, Willie	Brown, Davis
1908	U.S. Open	McLeod, Fred	Smith, Willie
1910	U.S. Open	Smith, Alex	McDermott, John
			Smith, McDonald
1911	British Open	Vardon, Harry	Massy, Arnaud
1911	U.S. Open	McDermott, John	Brady, Mike
			Simpson, George
1913	U.S. Open	Ouimet, Francis	Vardon, Harry
			Ray, Ted
1919	U.S. Open	Hagen, Walter	Brady, Mike
1921	British Open	Hutchison, Jock	Wethered, Roger (a)*
1923	U.S. Open	Jones, Bobby (a)	Cruickshank, Bobby
1925	U.S. Open	Macfarlane, Willie	Jones, Bobby (a)
1927	U.S. Open	Armour, Tommy	Cooper, Harry
1928	U.S. Open	Farrell, Johnny	Jones, Bobby (a)
1929	U.S. Open	Jones, Bobby (a)	Espinosa, Al
1931	U.S. Open	Burke, Billy	Von Elm, George
1933	British Open	Shute, Denny	Wood, Craig
1935	Masters	Sarazen, Gene	Wood, Craig
1939	U.S. Open	Nelson, Bryon	Wood, Craig
			Shute, Denny
1940	U.S. Open	Little, Lawson	Sarazen, Gene
1942	Masters	Nelson, Byron	Hogan, Ben
1946	U.S. Open	Mangrum, Lloyd	Nelson, Byron
			Ghezzi, Victor
1947	U.S. Open	Worsham, Lew	Snead, Sam
1949	British Open	Locke, Bobby	Bradshaw, Harry
1950	U.S. Open	Hogan, Ben	Mangrum, Lloyd
			Fazio, George

137

Year	Tournament	Winner	Runner-Up
1954	Masters	Snead, Sam	Hogan, Ben
1955	U.S. Open	Fleck, Jack	Hogan, Ben
1957	U.S. Open	Mayer, Dick	Middlecoff, Cary
1958	British Open	Thomson, Peter	Thomas, Dave
1961	PGA	Barber, Jerry	January, Don
1962	Masters	Palmer, Arnold	Player, Gary
			Finsterwald, Dow
1962	U.S. Open	Nicklaus, Jack	Palmer, Arnold
1963	British Open	Charles, Bob	Rodgers, Phil
1963	U.S. Open	Boros, Julius	Palmer, Arnold
			Cupit, Jacky
1965	U.S. Open	Player, Gary	Nagle, Kel
1966	Masters	Nicklaus, Jack	Jacobs, Tommy
			Brewer, Gay
1966	U.S. Open	Casper, Billy	Palmer, Arnold
1967	PGA	January, Don	Massengale, Don
1970	Masters	Casper, Billy	Littler, Gene
1970	British Open	Nicklaus, Jack	Sanders, Doug
1971	U.S. Open	Trevino, Lee	Nicklaus, Jack
1975	British Open	Watson, Tom	Newton, Jack
1975	U.S. Open	Graham, Lou	Mahaffey, John
1977	PGA	Wadkins, Lanny	Littler, Gene
1978	PGA	Mahaffey, John	Watson, Tom
			Pate, Jerry
1979	PGA	Graham, David	Crenshaw, Ben
1979	Masters	Zoeller, Fuzzy	Watson, Tom
			Sneed, Ed
1982	Masters	Stadler, Craig	Pohl, Dan
1984	U.S. Open	Zoeller, Fuzzy	Norman, Greg
1987	Masters	Mize, Larry	Norman, Greg
			Ballesteros, Seve
1987	PGA	Nelson, Larry	Wadkins, Lanny
1988	U.S. Open	Strange, Curtis	Faldo, Nick
1989	Masters	Faldo, Nick	Hoch, Scott
1989	British Open	Calcavecchia, Mark	Grady, Wayne
			Norman, Greg
1990	Masters	Faldo, Nick	Floyd, Ray
1990	U.S. Open	Irwin, Hale	Donald, Mike

* (a) denotes amateur status.

Playoff Listing by Tournament

Year	Course	Winner	Runner-Up

British Open

Year	Course	Winner	Runner-Up
1876	St. Andrews	Martin, R.	Strath, D.
1883	Musselburgh	Fernie, W.	Ferguson, R.
1889	Musselburgh	Park, W. Jr.	Kirkaldy, A.
1896	Muirfield	Vardon, H.	Taylor, J. H.
1911	Royal St. George's	Vardon, H.	Massy, A.
1921	St. Andrews	Hutchison, J.	Wethered, R. (a)
1933	St. Andrews	Shute, D.	Wood, C.
1949	Sandwich	Locke, B.	Bradshaw, H.
1958	Royal Lytham	Thomson, P.	Thomas, D.
1963	Royal Lytham	Charles, B.	Rodgers, P.
1970	St. Andrews	Nicklaus, J.	Sanders, D.
1975	Carnoustie	Watson, T.	Newton, J.
1989	Royal Troon	Calcavecchia, M.	Grady, W.
			Norman, G.

Masters

Year	Course	Winner	Runner-Up
1935	Augusta National	Sarazen, G.	Wood, C.
1942	Augusta National	Nelson, B.	Hogan, B.
1954	Augusta National	Snead, S.	Hogan, B.
1962	Augusta National	Palmer, A.	Player, G.
			Finsterwald, D.
1966	Augusta National	Nicklaus, J.	Jacobs, T.
			Brewer, G.
1970	Augusta National	Casper, B.	Littler, G.
1979	Augusta National	Zoeller, F.	Watson, T.
			Sneed, E.
1982	Augusta National	Stadler, C.	Pohl, D.
1987	Augusta National	Mize, L.	Norman, G.
			Ballesteros, S.
1989	Augusta National	Faldo, N.	Hoch, S.
1990	Augusta National	Faldo, N.	Floyd, R.

PGA

Year	Course	Winner	Runner-Up
1961	Olympia Fields	Barber, J.	January, D.
1967	Columbine	January, D.	Massengale, D.
1977	Pebble Beach	Wadkins, L.	Littler, G.
1978	Oakmont	Mahaffey, J.	Watson, T.
			Pate, J.
1979	Oakland Hills	Graham, D.	Crenshaw, B.
1987	PGA National	Nelson, L.	Wadkins, L.

Year	Course	Winner	Runner-Up
		U.S. Open	
1901	Myopia Hunt Club	Anderson, W.	Smith, A.
1903	Baltusrol	Anderson, W.	Brown, D.
1908	Myopia Hunt Club	McLeod, F.	Smith, W.
1910	Philadelphia	Smith, A.	McDermott, J.
			Smith, M.
1911	Chicago	McDermott, J.	Brady, M.
			Simpson, G.
1913	The Country Club	Ouimet, F.	Vardon, H.
			Ray, T.
1919	Brae Burn	Hagen, W.	Brady, M.
1923	Inwood	Jones, B. (a)	Cruickshank, B.
1925	Worcester	Macfarlane, W.	Jones, B. (a)
1927	Oakmont	Armour, T.	Cooper, H.
1928	Olympia Fields	Farrell, J.	Jones, B. (a)
1929	Winged Foot	Jones, B. (a)	Espinosa, A.
1931	Inverness	Burke, B.	Von Elm, G.
1939	Philadelphia	Nelson, B.	Wood, C.
			Shute, D.
1940	Canterbury	Little, L.	Sarazen, G.
1946	Canterbury	Mangrum, L.	Nelson, B.
			Ghezzi, V.
1947	St. Louis	Worsham, L.	Snead, S.
1950	Merion	Hogan, B.	Mangrum, L.
			Fazio, G.
1955	Olympic	Fleck, J.	Hogan, B.
1957	Inverness	Mayer, D.	Middlecoff, C.
1962	Oakmont	Nicklaus, J.	Palmer, A.
1963	The Country Club	Boros, J.	Palmer, A.
			Cupit, J.
1965	Bellerive	Player, G.	Nagle, K.
1966	Olympic	Casper, B.	Palmer, A.
1971	Merion	Trevino, L.	Nicklaus, J.
1975	Medinah	Graham, L.	Mahaffey, J.
1984	Winged Foot	Zoeller, F.	Norman, G.
1988	The Country Club	Strange, C.	Faldo, N.
1990	Medinah	Irwin, H.	Donald, M.

Playoff Listing Alphabetical by Winner

Tournament	Year	Winner	Runner-Up
U.S. Open	1901	Anderson, Willie	Smith, Alex
U.S. Open	1903	Anderson, Willie	Brown, Davis
U.S. Open	1927	Armour, Tommy	Cooper, Harry
PGA	1961	Barber, Jerry	January, Don

Tournament	Year	Winner	Runner-Up
U.S. Open	1963	Boros, Julius	Palmer, Arnold
			Cupit, Jacky
U.S. Open	1931	Burke, Billy	Von Elm, George
British Open	1989	Calcavecchia, Mark	Grady, Wayne
			Norman, Greg
U.S. Open	1966	Casper, Billy	Palmer, Arnold
Masters	1970	Casper, Billy	Littler, Gene
British Open	1963	Charles, Bob	Rodgers, Phil
Masters	1989	Faldo, Nick	Hoch, Scott
Masters	1990	Faldo, Nick	Floyd, Ray
U.S. Open	1928	Farrell, Johnny	Jones, Bobby (a)
British Open	1883	Fernie, Willie	Ferguson, Robert
U.S. Open	1955	Fleck, Jack	Hogan, Ben
PGA	1979	Graham, David	Crenshaw, Ben
U.S. Open	1975	Graham, Lou	Mahaffey, John
U.S. Open	1919	Hagen, Walter	Brady, Mike
U.S. Open	1950	Hogan, Ben	Mangrum, Lloyd
			Fazio, George
British Open	1921	Hutchison, Jock	Wethered, Roger (a)
U.S. Open	1990	Irwin, Hale	Donald, Mike
PGA	1967	January, Don	Massengale, Don
U.S. Open	1923	Jones, Bobby (a)	Cruickshank, Bobby
U.S. Open	1929	Jones, Bobby (a)	Espinosa, Al
U.S. Open	1940	Little, Lawson	Sarazen, Gene
British Open	1949	Locke, Bobby	Bradshaw, Harry
U.S. Open	1911	McDermott, John	Brady, Mike
			Simpson, George
U.S. Open	1925	Macfarlane, Willie	Jones, Barry (a)
U.S. Open	1908	McLeod, Fred	Smith, Willie
PGA	1978	Mahaffey, John	Watson, Tom
			Pate, Jerry
U.S. Open	1946	Mangrum, Lloyd	Nelson, Byron
			Ghezzi, Victor
British Open	1876	Martin, Robert	Strath, David
U.S. Open	1957	Mayer, Dick	Middlecoff, Cary
Masters	1987	Mize, Larry	Norman, Greg
			Ballesteros, Seve
Masters	1939	Nelson, Byron	Wood, Craig
Masters	1942	Nelson, Byron	Hogan, Ben
			Shute, Denny
PGA	1987	Nelson, Larry	Wadkins, Lanny
U.S. Open	1962	Nicklaus, Jack	Palmer, Arnold
Masters	1966	Nicklaus, Jack	Jacobs, Tommy
			Brewer, Gay
British Open	1970	Nicklaus, Jack	Sanders, Doug
U.S. Open	1913	Ouimet, Francis	Vardon, Harry
			Ray, Ted

Tournament	Year	Winner	Runner-Up
Masters	1962	Palmer, Arnold	Player, Gary
			Finsterwald, Dow
British Open	1889	Park, Willie, Jr.	Kirkaldy, Andrew
U.S. Open	1965	Player, Gary	Nagle, Kel
Masters	1935	Sarazen, Gene	Wood, Craig
British Open	1933	Shute, Denny	Wood, Craig
U.S. Open	1910	Smith, Alex	McDermott, John
			Smith, McDonald
Masters	1954	Snead, Sam	Hogan, Ben
Masters	1982	Stadler, Craig	Pohl, Dan
U.S. Open	1988	Strange, Curtis	Faldo, Nick
British Open	1958	Thomson, Peter	Thomas, Dave
U.S. Open	1971	Trevino, Lee	Nicklaus, Jack
British Open	1896	Vardon, Harry	Taylor, John H.
British Open	1911	Vardon, Harry	Massy, Arnaud
PGA	1977	Wadkins, Lanny	Littler, Gene
British Open	1975	Watson, Tom	Newton, Jack
U.S. Open	1947	Worsham, Lew	Snead, Sam
Masters	1979	Zoeller, Fuzzy	Watson, Tom
			Sneed, Ed
U.S. Open	1984	Zoeller, Fuzzy	Norman, Greg

Years with More Than One Playoff

1911	British Open, U.S. Open
1962	Masters, U.S. Open
1963	British Open, U.S. Open
1966	Masters, U.S. Open
1970	Masters, British Open
1975	British Open, U.S. Open
1979	Masters, PGA
1987	Masters, PGA
1989	Masters, British Open
1990	Masters, U.S. Open

Alphabetical Listing of
Individual Playoff Records

Anderson, Willie	2–0	Brady, Mike	0–2
Armour, Tommy	1–0	Brewer, Gay	0–1
Ballesteros, Seve	0–1	Brown, Davis	0–1
Barber, Jerry	1–0	Burke, Billy	1–0
Boros, Julius	1–0	Calcavecchia, Mark	1–0
Bradshaw, Harry	0–1	Casper, Billy	2–0

Charles, Bob	1-0	Mize, Larry	1-0
Cooper, Harry	0-1	Nagle, Kel	0-1
Crenshaw, Ben	0-1	Nelson, Byron	2-1
Cruickshank, Bobby	0-1	Nelson, Larry	1-0
Cupit, Jacky	0-1	Newton, Jack	0-1
Donald, Mike	0-1	Nicklaus, Jack	3-1
Espinoza, Al	0-1	Norman, Greg	0-3
Faldo, Nick	2-1	Ouimet, Francis	1-0
Fazio, George	0-1	Palmer, Arnold	1-3
Farrell, Johnny	1-0	Park, Willie, Jr.	1-0
Ferguson, Robert	0-1	Pate, Jerry	0-1
Fernie, Willie	1-0	Player, Gary	1-1
Finsterwald, Dow	0-1	Pohl, Dan	0-1
Fleck, Jack	1-0	Ray, Ted	0-1
Floyd, Ray	0-1	Rodgers, Phil	0-1
Ghezzi, Vic	0-1	Sanders, Doug	0-1
Graham, David	1-0	Sarazen, Gene	1-1
Graham, Lou	1-0	Shute, Denny	1-1
Hagen, Walter	1-0	Simpson, George	0-1
Hoch, Scott	0-1	Smith, Alex	1-1
Hogan, Ben	1-3	Smith, MacDonald	0-1
Hutchison, Jock	1-0	Smith, Willie	0-1
Irwin, Hale	1-0	Snead, Sam	1-1
Jacobs, Tommy	0-1	Sneed, Ed	0-1
January, Don	1-1	Stadler, Craig	1-0
Jones, Bobby	2-2	Strange, Curtis	1-0
Kirkaldy, Andrew	0-1	Strath, David	0-1
Little, Lawson	1-0	Taylor, John H.	0-1
Littler, Gene	0-2	Thomas, Dave	0-1
Locke, Bobby	1-0	Thomson, Peter	1-0
McDermott, John	1-1	Trevino, Lee	1-0
Macfarlane, Willie	1-0	Vardon, Harry	2-1
McLeod, Fred	1-0	Von Elm, George	0-1
Mahaffey, John	1-1	Wadkins, Lanny	1-1
Mangrum, Lloyd	1-1	Watson, Tom	1-2
Martin, Robert	1-0	Wethered, Roger	0-1
Massengale, Don	0-1	Wood, Craig	0-3
Massy, Arnaud	0-1	Worsham, Lew	1-0
Mayer, Dick	1-0	Zoeller, Fuzzy	2-0
Middlecoff, Cary	0-1		

Playoff Records

Longest Playoff

1931 U.S. Open, 72 holes. The tournament was conducted over 72 holes and the first 36 hole playoff resulted in another tie, requiring another 36 hole playoff, for a total 144 holes to determine the champion.

Most One-Sided Playoff

1929 U.S. Open, Bobby Jones defeated Al Espinoza by 23 shots.

Most Playoff Victories

3 by Jack Nicklaus (1962 U.S. Open, 1966 Masters, 1970 British Open).

Most Playoff Losses

Four players are tied with 3 losses: Ben Hogan (1942 Masters, 1954 Masters, 1955 U.S. Open); Greg Norman (1984 U.S. Open, 1987 Masters, 1989 British Open); Arnold Palmer (1962 U.S. Open, 1963 U.S. Open, 1966 U.S. Open); Craig Wood (1933 British Open, 1935 Masters, 1939 U.S. Open).

Courses Hosting Most Playoffs (excluding Augusta National)

4–St. Andrews (1876, 1921, 1933, 1970 British Open); 3–Oakmont cc (1927, 1962 U.S. Open, 1978 pga); 3–The Country Club (1913, 1963, 1988 U.S. Open).

Curious Facts About the Playoffs

- Brother defeats brother—Alex Smith defeated his brother MacDonald Smith (and Johnny McDermott) in the playoff for the 1910 U.S. Open.
- The playoff for the 1910 U.S. Open was held up one day as no competitive golf was permitted on Sunday.
- The playoff for the 1901 U.S. Open was delayed for two days as the course was reserved for members on weekends.
- Craig Wood was a loser in three consecutive playoffs: the 1933 British Open, the 1935 Masters, and the 1939 U.S. Open.
- First sudden-death playoff in a major championship—1977 pga Championship.
- Roger Wethered was the only amateur besides Bobby Jones to be involved in a major championship playoff—the 1921 British Open at St. Andrews.
- Willie Park, Jr., the winner in the 1889 playoff for the British Open, was the son of the first British Open champion, Willie Park, Sr.
- The playoff for the 1896 British Open title between Harry Vardon and John H. Taylor had to be postponed for one day as both professionals were committed to another professional tournament. After fulfilling their commitment, the playoff was completed.

- Only seven players have won two or more playoffs and only one player has won more than two:
Jack Nicklaus – 3
Willie Anderson – 2
Billy Casper – 2
Bobby Jones – 2
Byron Nelson – 2
Harry Vardon – 2
Fuzzy Zoeller – 2
Nick Faldo – 2

Appendix 2: Women

Playoff Listing by Tournament

Year	Course	Winner	Runner-Up
		U.S. Open	
1953	CC of Rochester	Rawls, Betsy	Pung, Jackie
1956	Northland CC	Cornelius, Kathy	McIntire, Barbara (a)
1964	San Diego CC	Wright, Mickey	Jessen, Ruth
1976	Rolling Green CC	Carner, JoAnne	Palmer, Sandra
1986	NCR CC	Geddes, Jane	Little, Sally
1987	Plainfield CC	Davies, Laura	Okamoto, Ayako
			Carner, Joanne
		LPGA	
1956	Forest Lake CC	Hagge, Marlene	Berg, Patty
1968	Pleasant Valley	Post, Sandra	Whitworth, Kathy
1970	Pleasant Valley	Englehorn, Shirley	Whitworth, Kathy
		Nabisco Dinah Shore	
1984	Mission Hills CC	Inkster, Juli	Bradley, Pat
1987	Mission Hills CC	King, Betsy	Sheehan, Patty
		du Maurier Classic	
1986	Board of Trade CC	Bradley, Pat	Okamoto, Ayako
		Titleholders	
1962	Augusta CC	Wright, Mickey	Jessen, Ruth
		Western Open	
1960	Beverly CC	Ziske, Joyce	Romack, Barbara

Chronological Playoff Listing

Year	Tournament	Winner	Runner-Up
1953	U.S. Open	Rawls, Betsy	Pung, Jackie
1956	U.S. Open	Cornelius, Kathy	McIntire, Barbara (a)
1956	LPGA	Hagge, Marlene	Berg, Patty
1960	Western Open	Ziske, Joyce	Romack, Barbara
1962	Titleholders	Wright, Mickey	Jessen, Ruth
1964	U.S. Open	Wright, Mickey	Jessen, Ruth
1968	LPGA	Post, Sandra	Whitworth, Kathy
1970	LPGA	Englehorn, Shirley	Whitworth, Kathy
1976	U.S. Open	Carner, JoAnne	Palmer, Sandra
1984	Dinah Shore	Inkster, Juli	Bradley, Pat
1986	du Maurier	Bradley, Pat	Okamoto, Ayako
1986	U.S. Open	Geddes, Jane	Little, Sally
1987	Dinah Shore	King, Betsy	Sheehan, Patty
1987	U.S. Open	Davies, Laura	Okamoto, Ayako
			Carner, JoAnne

Playoff Listing Alphabetical by Winner

Tournament	Year	Winner	Runner-Up
du Maurier	1986	Bradley, Pat	Okamoto, Ayako
U.S. Open	1976	Carner, JoAnne	Palmer, Sandra
U.S. Open	1956	Cornelius, Kathy	McIntire, Barbara (a)
U.S. Open	1987	Davies, Laura	Okamoto, Ayako
			Carner, JoAnne
LPGA	1970	Englehorn, Shirley	Whitworth, Kathy
U.S. Open	1986	Geddes, Jane	Little, Sally
LPGA	1956	Hagge, Marlene	Berg, Patty
Dinah Shore	1984	Inkster, Juli	Bradley, Pat
Dinah Shore	1987	King, Betsy	Sheehan, Patty
LPGA	1968	Post, Sandra	Whitworth, Kathy
U.S. Open	1953	Rawls, Betsy	Pung, Jackie
Titleholders	1962	Wright, Mickey	Jessen, Ruth
U.S. Open	1964	Wright, Mickey	Jessen, Ruth
Western Open	1960	Ziske, Joyce	Romack, Barbara

Individual Playoff Records

Berg, Patty	0–1	Cornelius, Kathy	1–0
Bradley, Pat	1–1	Davies, Laura	1–0
Carner, JoAnne	1–1	Englehorn, Shirley	1–0

Geddes, Jane	1–0	Post, Sandra	1–0
Hagge, Marlene	1–0	Pung, Jackie	0–1
Inkster, Juli	1–0	Rawls, Betsy	1–0
Jessen, Ruth	0–2	Romack, Barbara	0–1
King, Betsy	1–0	Sheehan, Patty	0–1
Little, Sally	0–1	Whitworth, Kathy	0–2
McIntire, Barbara (a)	0–1	Wright, Mickey	2–0
Okamoto, Ayako	0–2	Ziske, Joyce	1–0
Palmer, Sandra	0–1		

Bibliography

Books

Alfano, Pete. *Grand Slam*. New York: Stadia Sports Publishing, 1973.

Armour, Tommy. *How to Play Your Best Golf All the Time*. New York: Simon and Schuster, 1953.

Barkow, Al. *Gettin' to the Dance Floor*. New York: Atheneum, 1986.

Bartlett's World Golf Encyclopedia. Michael Bartlett, ed. New York: Bantam Books, 1973.

Edmonson, Jolee. *The Woman Golfer's Catalogue*. New York: Stein and Day, 1980.

The Encyclopedia of Golf. Nevin H. Gibson, ed. New York; A. S. Barnes and Company, 1964.

Flaherty, Tom. *The U.S. Open (1895–1965)*. New York: E. P. Dutton, 1966.

Gibson, Nevin, and Tommy Kouzmanoff. *Golf's Greatest Shots by the World's Greatest Players*. Great Neck, N.Y.: Todd & Honeywell, 1981.

Jones, Robert T., Jr., and O. B. Keeler. *Down the Fairway*. New York: Minton, Balch, 1927.

LPGA 1988 Player Guide.

LPGA 1989 Player Guide.

McCormack, Mark H. *The Wonderful World of Professional Golf*. New York: Atheneum, 1973.

Martin, H. B. *Fifty Years of American Golf*. Argosy-Antiquarian, 1966.

_____. *St. Andrews Golf Club, 1888–1963*.

Morrison, Ian. *Great Moments in Golf*. New York: Gallery Books, 1987.

_____. *100 Greatest Golfers*. Greenwhich, Conn.: Brompton Books, 1988.

Nickerson, Elinor. *Golf: A Woman's History*. Jefferson, N.C.: McFarland, 1986.

Park, Willie, Jr. *The Game of Golf*.

The PGA Championship, 1916–1984. George Peper, ed. The PGA of America, 1984.

Price, Charles. *A Golf Story*. New York: Atheneum, 1986.

Salmond, J. B. *The Story of the R & A*. London: MacMillan, 1956.

Sarazen, Gene. *Thirty Years of Championship Golf*. New York: Prentice-Hall, 1950.

Sommers, Robert. *The U.S. Open*. New York: Atheneum, 1987.

Vardon, Harry. *My Golfing Life*, from *Vardon on Golf*. Herbert Warren Wind and Robert Macdonald, eds. Aika Inc. 1989.

Williams, Michael. *Grand Slam*. Secaucus, N.J.: Chartwell Books, 1988.
_____. *History of Golf*. Secaucus, N.J.: Chartwell Books, 1987.
Wind, Herbert Warren. *Following Through*. New York: Ticknor & Fields, 1985.
_____. *The Story of American Golf*. New York: Alfred A. Knopf, 1975.
The World Atlas of Golf. Mitchell Beazley Publishers. Great Britain, 1976.

Periodicals

Golf Digest. February 1976, pp. 26, 28.
Golf Illustrated. June 1988, pp. 42–46. "The Ref of Refs"
Golf Journal. September 1976, pp. 6–11. "A Rolling Open Goes to Gundy."
_____. May/June 1985, pp. 27–32. "A Figure from History."
_____. September 1986, pp. 5–10. "An Unforgettable Women's Open."
_____. July 1987, pp. 16–20. "Muirfield: An Historical Restrospective."
_____. July 1987, pp. 28–32. "The Fitful Beginnings of the LPGA."
_____. September 1987, pp. 5–10. "Another Country Heard From."
_____. August 1988, pp. 5–13. "The Open: A Tradition Continues."
_____. October 1989, pp. 19–24. "A Quiet Growing Marketplace."
_____. July 1989, pp. 24–28. "A Sixth Would Be Sweet, Indeed."
The Golf Reporter. April 1989, pp. 12–16. "The Rest Is History."
Golf Magazine. May 1984, pp. 117–19. "Heeeere's Juli!"
_____. Yearbook, February 1985.
_____. June 1988, pp. 69–76. "Extra! Extra!"
Golf World. July 3, 1953, pp. 8–9. "Great Victory for Betsy Rawls."
_____. June 29, 1956, p. 8. "Marlene Champion."
_____. August 3, 1956, pp. 3, 6. "New Open Queen."
_____. July 1, 1960, p. 13. "Ziske Wins Playoff."
_____. May 4, 1962, pp. 3, 6, 22. "Mickey Repeats."
_____. July 17, 1964, pp. 6–8. "Mickey Wins 4th Open in Playoff."
_____. September 9, 1966, pp. 2, 3, 6, 19, 20.
_____. June 28, 1968, pp. 4–5, 8. "Sandra Post Wins LPGA Crown."
_____. April 21, 1970, pp. 6–8, 33–38. "California Stars Dominate the Masters."
_____. June 23, 1970, pp. 6–7. "The LPGA Has a Tiger on Its Tour."
_____. July 16, 1976, pp. 36–40. "Carner Passes Survival Course."
_____. July 18, 1986, pp. 14–19. "She'll Remember This One."
_____. August 1, 1986, pp. 14–17. "Another Major Success.."
_____. August 14, 1987, pp. 24–33. "Good Day for a Walk."
_____. June 24, 1988, pp. 24–44. "A Superstar Now!"
_____. April 14, 1989, pp. 32–47. "Just in the Nick of Time."
_____. April 13, 1990, pp. 34–46. "Repeating History."
_____. June 8, 1990, pp. 16–23. Remembering the One That Got Away."
_____. June 22, 1990, pp. 16–31. "Hale to the Champion."
PGA. February 1989, pp. 22–25, 56, 63. "Pressure Points." Joe Gordon.
USGA *Golf Journal*. August 1964, pp. 7–10. "Mickey Wright and the Queens of Golf."

USGA Journal. August, 1953, pp. 14–15. "Miss Rawls New Open Champion."

USGA Journal and Turf Management. August 1957, pp. 5–7. "A Girl's Reunion at Women's Open."

Index